starting out:
defensive play

ANGUS DUNNINGTON

EVERYMAN CHESS

Gloucester Publishers plc   www.everymanchess.com

First published in 2005 by Gloucester Publishers plc (formerly Everyman Publishers plc), Northburgh House, 10 Northburgh Street, London EC1V 0AT

British Library Cataloguing-in-Publication Data
A catalogue record for this book is available from the British Library.

ISBN 1 85744 368 3

Distributed in North America by The Globe Pequot Press, P.O Box 480, 246 Goose Lane, Guilford, CT 06437-0480.

All other sales enquiries should be directed to Everyman Chess, Northburgh House, 10 Northburgh Street, London EC1V 0AT
tel: 020 7253 7887; fax: 020 7490 3708
email: info@everymanchess.com
website: www.everymanchess.com

EVERYMAN CHESS SERIES (formerly Cadogan Chess)
Chief Advisor: Garry Kasparov
Commissioning editor: Byron Jacobs
General editor: John Emms

Typeset and edited by First Rank Publishing, Brighton.
Cover design by Horatio Monteverde.
Production by Navigator Guides.
Printed and bound in the US by Versa Press.

Contents

Introduction

Defending is obviously not the most interesting part of the game – we'd much prefer to be on the right side of a Tal-like, spectacular mating attack or grinding out a technical win an ending in the style of Ulf Andersson. This would certainly be more fun than soaking up unwelcome pressure as a result of our opponent entertaining himself with a disruptive pawn sacrifice right in front of our castled king. But a harsh reality of chess is that – as in life – we don't always get what we want; in fact we too often get what we don't want. During the course of a tournament or a season of club matches it would be rare indeed for a player not to experience at least a couple of times the discomfort caused by having to defend against a brutal attack or a long-term pull, for example. It would be useful, then, to at least give the subject of defending some consideration away from the board as part of our general preparation.

The examples in this book are aimed at helping the reader better appreciate that defending is an inevitable and crucial part of the game, that unless we make a conscious effort to address the subject we will suffer from the cumulative loss of half-points and points that we let slip through our fingers. After more than twenty years writing about chess I understand that it is not possible to provide a fool-proof guide to this or that aspect of the game in a single book. Consequently I have worked along the lines of some of my previous books, selecting practical examples almost at random from a database. The chapter headings and categories in which the games fall are of minimal importance. My intention was to steer the reader in the right direction with a collection of examples of the kind of play we are likely to encounter throughout our chess career, the emphasis on the role of defence. Nothing earth-shattering, rather a series of realistic but instructive games accompanied by what I hope is some good advice.

Incidentally, playing solidly and sensibly when the situation so dictates doesn't by any means restrict you to a lifetime of draws. Against lots of players steering the game to a level, ostensibly simple situation will in fact offer decent winning chances, as some people just won't share. This is because while the opponent is still trying – or not trying – to face the reality that there is no longer an initiative or attack from which an advantage might materialise he is more likely to blunder in his efforts to avoid acquiescing to a draw.

TIP: Coming to the end of a successful period of defence doesn't mean we should no longer contemplate earning the full point.

□ V.Bologan ■ A.Dreev

Poikovsky 2002

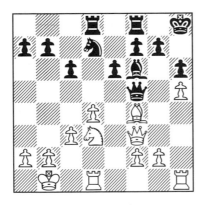

Diagram 1
Position after 20 Qf3

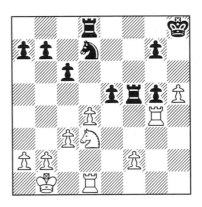

Diagram 2
Position after 26...e5

White stands better because an attack on the enemy king looks to be quicker in the making. However, stern defence from Black should be enough to maintain the balance.

20...Bg5!

Eliminating a potentially dangerous piece is a good place to start.

6

21 Bxg5 Qxg5!

It might seem tempting to further simplify with 21...Qxf3?!, which also damages White's structure, but after 22 gxf3 hxg5 23 Rdg1 f6 24 f4 Black is struggling, while White has anyway been able to drum up an initiative.

22 g4 f5

Another logical move that many of us would need some convincing to play, but Black cannot sit idly by while White marches forward after making way for f2-f4 etc.

23 Qf4

White has given up on trying for an advantage with the queens on so adopts a fresh approach. Alternatively, 23 Rdg1 fxg4 24 Qxg4 Qxg4 25 Rxg4 Rf5 is equal.

23...fxg4!

In the event of 23...Qxg4?! White has the surprisingly strong 24 Qc7! with the idea of bringing the knight to f4 as well as hoovering up Black's queenside pawns. The text guarantees an exchange of queens.

24 Qxg5 hxg5 25 Rhg1 Rf5 26 Rxg4 e5 (Diagram 2)

26...Nf6 27 Rgg1 looks equal but Black understandably wishes to rid himself of the weak e-pawn while he has the chance.

27 Rdg1

27 Re1 Nf6! (27...exd4 28 Rxd4) 28 Rxe5 Rxe5 29 Nxe5 Nxg4 30 Nf7+ Kh7 31 Nxd8 Nxf2 is given by Lukacs, who continues 32 Kc2 g4 33 Kd2 g3 34 Ke2 Nd3 35 Kf3 Nxb2 36 Nxb7 Kh6 37 Na5 Na4 38 Nxc6 Nxc3 with equality. The text should also lead to a draw pretty soon, but it turns out that White isn't yet ready to split the point.

27...Nf6 28 Rxg5 Rxg5 29 Rxg5 exd4 30 Ne5

30 Kc2 dxc3 31 bxc3 is level.

30...Kh7 31 Kc2?

31 Nf7! Rd7 32 Ne5 is tantamount to a draw offer, while Black might be tempted to play on with 31...Rf8 32 Nd6 d3 33 Kc1 b6, but White prefers to be more positive. Unfortunately for him this is a serious mistake.

31...dxc3 32 bxc3 Ne4 (Diagram 3)

Suddenly White's uncompromising attempt at a slightly more active set-up has allowed Black to pounce, the result being the loss of a pawn.

Consequently White has been dealt (has dealt himself) a severe psychological blow, seeing his opponent's original careful, accurate defence turn to standard simplification as the ending approaches and then, from nowhere, one mini-tactic puts Black in the driving seat. It is interesting just how quickly White now collapses.

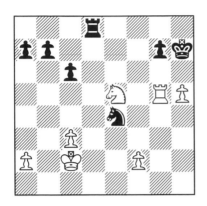

| **Diagram 3** | **Diagram 4** |
| Position after 32...Ne4 | Position after 36...Nd3 |

33 Rg4

After 33 Rf5 Rd2+ 34 Kb3 Rxf2 the h-pawn will soon be toast.

33...Rd2+ 34 Kb3 Nxf2 35 Rb4

Other than outright blunders, you'd do well to find a better way to lose than what you're about to see.

35...Rd5 36 Nc4??

Something like 36 Nf7 is forced, when 36...Nd3 anyway prevents Rxb7 in view of the fork on c5, leaving White struggling in the ending.

36...Nd3 0-1 (Diagram 4)

About a half-dozen moves ago White needed to come to terms with the fact that his opponent deserved to draw. Now it's time to resign because he's about to lose an exchange. All Black did in this game was defend sensibly and keep his wits about him in case a fortuitous opportunity arose.

Chess is not an easy game, and defence is certainly not an easy subject to get to grips with, but if we adopt a sensible, common-sense approach as part of our preparation, then performance will improve. That you have already acknowledged that defence merits special time and effort is a good start, and augurs well for those encounters with players whose 'work' is limited exclusively to how much of the latest opening theory they can regurgitate.

Good Luck!

Angus Dunnington

Hightae (Scotland),

July 2005

Active Defence

The age of the computer has seen powerful analysis engines find flaws (some more serious than others) in many so-called masterpieces, yet these games (Tal's spring to mind) hold great instructional and entertainment value nonetheless. While we continue to compete in matches and tournaments against our fellow man and woman, active defence will remain a practical weapon rather than a search for truth.

Don't Be Afraid To Sacrifice

If the only way to steer the game away from a prospectless, unpleasant course is a sacrifice of material that still leaves us much worse but with a fighting chance, then so be it. Often such possibilities present themselves only when the dark clouds are beginning to gather overhead, and failure to face facts and recognise and subsequently grasp these opportunities is tantamount to resignation. Better to throw some obstacles out – both on the board and in the mind of the opposition.

In the example below Black is faced with a standard aggressive theme that threatens to push him off the board, so decisive action is called for.

□ **P.Tregubov** ■ **H.Hamdouchi**

Belfort 2002

1 d4 e6 2 c4 c5 3 d5 exd5 4 cxd5 d6 5 Nc3 g6 6 Nf3 Bg7 7 Nd2 a6?! 8 a4 Nd7 9 e4 Ngf6 10 Be2 0-0 11 0-0 Re8 12 f4 Rb8 13 Kh1! c4

If you value your pawns then this is not the defence for you! Quiet play from Black here would merely invite White to steamroll through the centre soon with e4-e5, so Black gets his queenside counterplay going without delay. The point of the text is to meet 14 Bxc4 with 14...Nc5, e.g. 15 Qf3 Bg4 16 Qg3 b5! 17 axb5 axb5 with a complex position.

14 e5!?

White prefers to mould the complications to his own choosing.

14...dxe5 15 Nxc4 e4 16 f5 (Diagram 1)

Instead of accepting the gift White also offered a pawn in order to unleash the c1-bishop and look menacing on the f-file. Stohl offers the sensible 16 Be3!? as an alternative, e.g. 16...b6 17 Nd6 Re7 18 Rc1 Nc5 19 Nxc8 Rxc8 20 b4 Nd3 21 Bxd3 exd3 22 Qxd3 Ng4 23 Bg1, or 16...b5 17 axb5 axb5 18 Na5, awarding a clear advantage to White in either case. But the text is more aggressive and puts Black in a more awkward predicament.

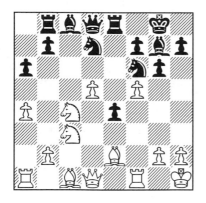

Diagram 1
Position after 16 f5

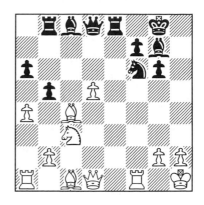

Diagram 2
Position after 20...b5!

16...e3!?

The '!?' here is from Stohl, who gives 16...Nb6 17 fxg6 hxg6 (17...fxg6 18 Bg5) 18 Nxb6 Qxb6 19 a5 Qc5 20 Bg5 Nd7 21 Bf4 as clearly better for White. This is indeed true, although White's lead after 21...Ra8 would probably be smaller than might have been the case after the uncompromising ...e4-e3. But Hamdouchi – like many GMs – is not in the habit of passive play and giving the opposition carte blanche to pile on the pressure, especially if he can generate some activity of his own. Black's plan runs the risk of shedding too many pawns but at least White is forced to engage in some way rather than leisurely add to the initiative. And herein lies the secret to active defence in instances such as the one we have here – given that both options most probably lead to difficulties, if the active option offers greater practical chances of uncompromising resistance along with a greater possibility of a quicker defeat, then many players prefer this to a less promising, opponent-friendly yet 'mathematically' more accurate course.

17 Nxe3

17 Bxe3? makes no sense as 17...b5 18 axb5 axb5 19 Bf4 bxc4 20 Bxb8 Nxb8 helps only Black.

17...Ne5 18 fxg6

18 Bd2!? Bd7 19 Qb3 maintains the tension.

18...hxg6 19 Nc4

It is natural to challenge the well placed knight, although this falls in with Black's strategy. With this in mind Stohl suggests 19 Qb3! with the idea of meeting 19...Neg4 with 20 Bxg4 Nxg4 21 Nxg4 Bxg4 22 Bf4 and a healthy extra pawn for which Black's bishop pair doesn't compensate.

19...Nxc4 20 Bxc4 b5! (Diagram 2)

The consistent follow-up to Black's 'pawns get in the way' philosophy.

 TIP: If you don't have anywhere near enough play for a pawn it makes sense to throw another on the fire if this means earning yourself a bigger share of the play.

21 axb5 axb5 22 Bxb5

22 Nxb5 Ne4!? 23 Qf3 Bf5 24 g4? Nd2! is the kind of tricky line Black will have had in mind. Instead White collects the second pawn in the more conventional way, after which Black puts his faith in the open lines his forces enjoy.

22...Bd7 23 Bxd7

23 Bc4 Rb4 is another alternative but White, understandably, trades off a pair of pieces while he can. Given the extra material (two passed pawns) White now seeks to remove the queens, too.

23...Qxd7 24 Qa4

From here the queen covers e4 while offering a trade, but Stohl's 24 Qf3 looks good, e.g. 24...Rb4 (24...Ng4!?) 25 Rd1, when the desired 25...Ne4 26 Nxe4 Rbxe4 meets with the effective 27 Ra8!, decisively rendering Black's army powerless.

24...Qb7 25 Qa7

Note how White sees the coming exchange as a game winner. Otherwise he might have considered 25 Qc4 Rbc8 26 Qd3.

25...Ne4! (Diagram 3)

Black has been waiting to launch his knight, and this advance is surprisingly useful because in forcing the removal of its opposite number Black is better able to attack the extra pawns.

26 Nxe4 Rxe4 27 h3

27 Qxb7 Rxb7 28 Rd1 Be5 29 g3 Reb4 might be an improvement for White. However, we have a not uncommon situation here in that both players seem to be under the illusion that Black's vigorous defence has been effective, and the next few moves see the game drift away from White.

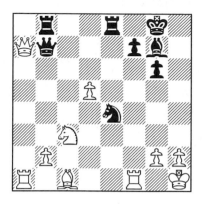

Diagram 3
Position after 25...Ne4!

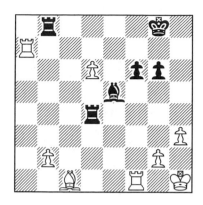

Diagram 4
Position after 30...f6

27...Be5 28 Ra5 Rd4 29 d6

29 Be3 Qxa7 (Stohl offers 29...Rb4!?) 30 Rxa7 Rxd5 31 Raxf7 Bxb2 sees White emerge with a 2-1 majority but Black's defensive task is eased considerably by the localisation of the struggle on the kingside.

29...Qxa7 30 Rxa7 f6 (Diagram 4) 31 d7

I wonder how early Black had noticed the variation 31 Be3 Rxd6 32 b4 Rxb4! 33 Bc5 Rf4! 34 Rb1 Rd8 with a completely level game. Meanwhile 32 Bc5 Rd2 33 b4 Rbd8, intending to meet 34 b5 with 34...R8d5, maintains Black's activity.

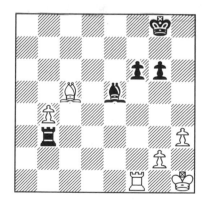

Diagram 5
Position after 35...Rb3

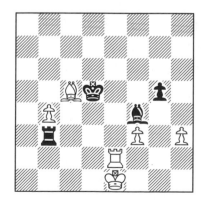

Diagram 6
Position after 48 Ke1

31...Rd8 32 Be3 R4xd7 33 Rxd7 Rxd7 34 b4 Rd3 35 Bc5 Rb3 (Diagram 5)

While Black has not recouped the total investment he has managed to find optimum posts for his remaining two pieces, and the passed pawn is well monitored. No doubt there have been improvements for White along the way, but White's play has been quite reasonable and, moreover, any inaccuracies can be attributed at least in some part to the pressure created by Black's confident, uncompromising defence that began with 16...e3, when Hamdouchi was not prepared to take what he considered to be a futile route.

36 Kg1

Thanks to the dominating e5-bishop White must bring his king out of the corner.

36...Kf7 37 Rd1 Ke6

Black's bind of sorts also affords him the more active king.

38 Kf2 g5 39 Ke2 f5

This advance is indicative of Black's confidence as 39...Rg3 40 Kf1 Rb3 puts the onus on White to find something else constructive.

40 Rd3 Rb2+ 41 Rd2 Rb3 42 Kd1

42 Ra2 Kd5 43 Be7 g4 explains Black's kingside 'expansion' because the subsequent try with 44 h4 gives Black something of his own to bite on after 44...f4 etc.

42...f4 43 Re2 Kd5 44 Kc2 Rb2+ 45 Kd3 Rb3+ 46 Kd2 f3

A simple route to a draw is 46...Bd4 47 Be7 (47 Bxd4 Kxd4 and the b-pawn drops) 47...Rb2+ 48 Kd1 Rb1+ etc.

47 gxf3

47 Rf2? fxg2 48 Rxg2 Rb2+ and Black wins.

47...Bf4+

47...Rxf3 48 Re3 Bf4 49 Ke2 Bxe3 50 Kxf3 Bxc5 51 bxc5 Kxc5 52 Kg4 Kd6 53 Kxg5 Ke7 also draws.

48 Ke1 ½-½ (Diagram 6)

After 48...Rxf3 the h-pawn falls. With absolute best play it is quite possible that Black's active defence was not the most accurate choice available. However, from a practical point of view there is a strong argument for it being the best option because in so many instances Black had either plenty of activity or excellent drawing chances. I am sure most strong players would find such circumstances preferable to a passive alternative.

Breaking the Bind

One of the most unpleasant situations is defending a position in which you have a definite, exploitable weakness, often a weak pawn that becomes a target or an important square over which you have little or no influence. Indeed it can be torture defending against constant occupation of a hole in your half of the board, which is why strong players are not afraid to investigate radical means with which to wrest control from the opposition. Here is an example of the temporary pawn sacrifice which, to many players, does seem radical, yet, for the likes of Shirov, is merely a means to an end that avoids passivity.

□ P.Leko ■ A.Shirov
Candidates semi-final, Dortmund 2002

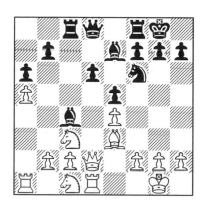

Diagram 7
Position after 15 Nc1

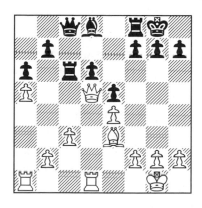

Diagram 8
Position after 24 Qxd5

No prizes for guessing Black's problem here. Of course there are two related problems, namely the backward d6-pawn and the accompanying weak square directly in front of it. Depending on which minor pieces stay in play life can become very difficult for Black, the worst combination (for Black) being a knight for White and the dark-squared bishop for Black. Even a rook ending would be quite uncomfortable as White could gang up on the d-pawn and shore up the queenside with c2-c3 if necessary. In E.Flacker-U.Rohde, Germany 1993 Black returned his bishop to the fold, but after 15...Be6 16 Bb6 Qe8 17 Nd3 Rc4 18 f3 Nd7 19 Bf2 f5 20 b3 Rc8 21 Nb4 White's control over d5 should have outweighed Black's attempts at activity.

15...d5!

We could have expected Shirov to strive for freedom. In fact this sacrifice was a theoretical novelty at the time of the game. The earlier heavyweight game E.Geller-V.Tukmakov, Yerevan 1982 developed as follows: 15...Rc6 16 Nd3 Bxd3 17 Qxd3 Qd7 18 Bg5 Nh5 19 Be3 Nf6 and now White took an interesting (rather than direct) route to d5 in 20 Na4 Qe6 21 Nb6 Bd8 22 Nd5 Qc8 23 c3 Nxd5 24 Qxd5 **(Diagram 8)**.

This is not the kind of position we want to be defending. Even now the d5-square is still proving useful for White, the d6-pawn remains a liability and Black has the inferior minor piece. Nor is there a way in which Black might be able to inconvenience his opponent. All in all a thankless defensive task. With this kind of position in mind Shirov manages to come up with an effective plan.

16 Bb6!

Hitting the queen troubles Black more than the compromising 16 exd5 Bb4 17 Bb6 Bxc3! 18 Qxc3 Qd6, when Black will regain the pawn with a comfortable position.

16...Qe8!

An accurate follow-up that Black will have had ready when he decided to venture 15...d5. The point behind putting the queen here rather than d7 is to avoid a pin on the d-file in the event of ...d5-d4 to hit the knight. After 16...Qd7 17 b3 d4 18 bxc4 Rxc4 19 Nd5 Nxd5 20 exd5 Rfc8 21 Qe1 Qxd5 22 c3 the piece outweighs the pawns thanks to both the pin on the d-file and the one on the e-file that comes into play after 22...Rxc3 23 Ne2 Rc2 24 Nxd4 etc. Similarly, White can exploit the location of the queen on the d-file after 17...Bb4 18 bxc4 d4 19 N1a2, when 19...Bxc3 20 Nxc3 Rxc4 21 Na2 Rfc8 22 c3 is clearly better for White.

17 exd5

This time 17 b3 can be met with 17...d4 18 bxc4 dxc3 19 Qxc3 (19 Qd3 Qc6) 19...Nxe4 20 Qxe5 Rxc4 and Black looks better. There is also 17...Bb4 18 bxc4 Nxe4 19 Nxe4 Bxd2 20 Nxd2 dxc4 21 Ne4 Qe7 with an interesting queen versus three pieces scenario.

17...Bb4 (Diagram 9)

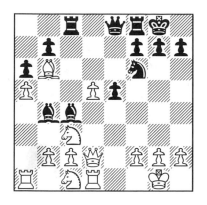

Diagram 9
Position after 17...Bb4

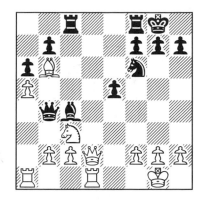

Diagram 10
Position after 20...Qxb4

For the pawn Black has managed to generate some activity and undermine the defence of d5. In an ideal world Black wants to force the
(re)capture of the pawn and emerge with at least an equal game thanks
to his extra centre pawn. Of course Black is happy should be content
with equality because had he not played the uncompromising ...d6-d5
he would face a difficult middlegame. In the diagram position White
has 18 Nd3, when the forcing 18...Bxc3 19 Qxc3 Nxd5 20 Qxe5 Nxb6 21
axb6 Bxd3 22 Qxe8 Rfxe8 leads to a level ending, e.g. 23 Rxd3 (23 cxd3
Rc2) 23...Rxc2 24 Rd7 Rb8 etc.

18 d6!

White tries for more, putting the onus on Black to demonstrate a route
to calmer waters.

18...Qd7

Black doesn't rush into ...Bxc3 so that – with the queen occupying d7 –
...Ne4 is a threat. In fact White will indeed have to return the d-pawn,
so it is a matter of how he allows the points score to be restored and
whether he can hold on to some kind of edge.

19 Nd3

19 Qe3 Bxd6 20 Nb3 Qc6 is fine for Black, so White tries another idea.

19...Qxd6 20 Nxb4 Qxb4 (Diagram 10)

Black has come a long way in only the five moves since we started! The
backward d6-pawn has gone, and with it the weakness on d5, while
Black even enjoys the more actively posted forces. Mission accom-

plished.

21 Ne4!

21 Qc1 Bb5 22 Ra3 Bc6 has been evaluated as equal by Ftacnik but Black seems to have a slight pull. The text is an admission from White that Black's pawn sac has worked, inviting a couple of trades that steer the game to easy equality.

21...Qxd2 22 Nxf6+ gxf6 23 Rxd2 Be6 24 f3 Rc4

The doubled pawns mean nothing here as White is unable to get at them. Nor is there a way in for either player's rooks.

25 c3 Kg7 26 Re1 Rfc8 27 Kf2 h5 28 Red1 Ra4 29 Rd6 ½-½

This was yet another example in which the hero's play seemed simple and logical, but the hard part was in pushing the d-pawn in the first place. Of course chess knowledge is an accumulation of all sorts of things, so having seen Shirov's treatment here we should now be looking out for similar opportunities each time we find ourselves in this kind of situation.

Active Defence

Hitting back at the opponent when under pressure is not restricted to the opening or middlegame. In the next example Karpov suddenly turns up the heat in a bid to unsettle his opponent.

☐ **A.Karpov** ■ **B.Gelfand**

Dos Hermanas 1997

White is a pawn down, his king has unwelcome company and his knight is in a world of its own. What better circumstances could there be to go on the offensive?

41 h5!

Not happy about having his king facing Black's pawn mass, Karpov elects to take matters into his own hands.

41...Kh7 42 Ra6 Rc1 43 Kh4

The king prepares to come to g5, where it can hide on the 'wrong' side of the pawns to help stir up some trouble for Black's king. With correct play Black should be winning, but this would have been a near certainty anyway had White not been so pro-active. At least now Black is faced with potentially hazardous defensive problems of his own as well as working out how best to see home his advantage. Already, then, Karpov has succeeded in significantly improving his chances.

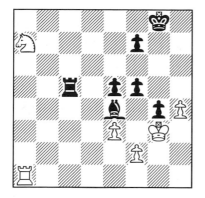

Diagram 11
Position after 40...f5

Diagram 12
Position after 44...Bf3!!

43...Rf1

Not a blunder as such, but with the text Black nevertheless misses out on an opportunity to strike before the pressure mounts. After 43...Rh1+ 44 Kg5 there is 44...Bf3!! **(Diagram 12)**. Then 45 Rf6 g3! adds a mate possibility on h5 to the threat of promotion, while 45 Rd6 Rxh5+! 46 Kf6 (46 Kxh5 g3+) 46...f4 47 exf4 exf4 is also decisive. This leaves 45 Kf6 f4 46 exf4 exf4, e.g. 47 Ra3 g3! (47...Rf1!?) 48 fxg3 fxg3 49 Rxf3 g2 50 Rg3 Rf1+ 51 Ke7 g1Q 52 Rxg1 Rxg1 53 Nc6 (53 Kxf7 Rg7+) 53...f5 etc.

Of course the fact that a super-GM such as Gelfand has difficulty latching on to the correct line highlights the practical worth of White's offensive.

44 Rf6 Rxf2 45 Nc8! (Diagram 13)

The knight is (finally) ready for action. Obviously Black has no problems as far as pawns are concerned, but his king is in danger of coming unstuck because the rook and bishop are busy trying to generate a new queen. That Black has these concerns at all is good news for White.

45...Bd5?

The obvious 45...Rh2+ 46 Kg5 g3 47 Rxf7+ Kg8 (47...Kh8 48 Ne7 Bd5 49 Ng6+ Kg8 50 Rc7 Bf7 51 Kf6 and mate is inevitable) 48 Kf6 is tantamount to a help-mate, e.g. 48...f4 49 Ne7+ Kh8 50 Ng6+ Bxg6 51

Rf8+ Kh7 52 hxg6+ etc. The text avoids this but, unfortunately for Black, is good enough only for a draw. However, despite the signs that the full point was drifting away, there was still a way for Black to win: 45...Kg7! 46 Kg5 g3 47 h6+ Kf8 48 Rd6 (48 Nd6 Ke7) 48...Ke8 49 Rd1 (49 h7 Rh2) 49...Bc2 50 h7 (50 Rg1 f4) 50...Rh2 51 Nd6+ (51 Rd2 g2) 51...Kd7! (51...Kf8 52 Rg1) 52 Rd2 g2 53 Nxf5+ Ke8 54 h8Q+ Rxh8 55 Ng7+ Ke7 56 Rxg2 f6+ 57 Kg4 Be4 **(Diagram 14)**.

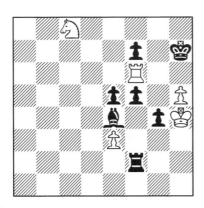

Diagram 13	Diagram 14
Position after 45 Nc8!	Position after 57...Be4

It's been a long and winding route but Black has emerged with a decisive advantage, e.g. 58 Rg3 Kf7 59 Nh5 Bc2 and the struggle is over. To find a way through this kind of line at the board is a mammoth task for anyone, so Black can be forgiven for letting the win slip through his fingers. The text comes to the aid of the king but it turns out that White has more than one string to his bow, meaning that Black has simply lost a vital tempo.

46 Nd6 Rh2+ 47 Kg5 g3 48 Nxf5 (Diagram 15)

48...Be6

Black must be careful. Again pushing the pawn leads to trouble: 48...g2 49 Rh6+ Kg8 50 Kf6 and now 50...g1Q sees Black mated after 51 Ne7+ Kf8 52 Rh8+. In the event of 48...Rxh5+ 49 Kxh5 g2 White's problem is getting the rook to the g-file or finding a suitable distraction: 50 Rh6+ Kg8 51 Ne7+ Kf8 52 Nf5 f6 53 Rh8+ Kf7 (53...Bg8 54 Nh6) 54 Rh7+ Ke6 55 Ng7+ with a draw.

49 Nxg3 Rg2 50 Kh4 Rh2+ 51 Kg5 Rg2 52 Kh4 Kg7

Black is not ready to shake hands yet.

53 Rf1

53 Rf3 looks okay, too.

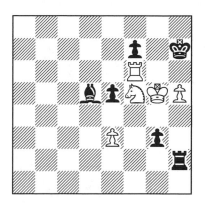

Diagram 15
Position after 48 Nxf5

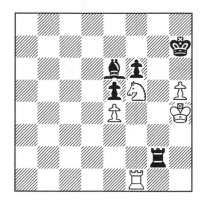

Diagram 16
Position after 57 e4

53...Rh2+ 54 Kg5 Rg2 55 Kh4 f6 56 Nf5+ Kh7 57 e4 (Diagram 16)

By now White has re-established himself. Even the material is level, but Black anyway goes through the motions for a few more moves.

57...Bd7

An entertaining alternative is 57...Re2 58 Nd6 Re3 when White skates on thin ice yet survives nonetheless: 59 Rxf6 Rh3+ 60 Kg5 Rg3+ 61 Kh4 Rg4+ 62 Kh3 Rg6+ 63 Rxe6 Rxe6 64 Nf5 etc.

58 h6 Re2

58...Rg5 59 Ne7 is level.

59 Nd6 Kg6 60 Kg3 Re3+ 61 Rf3 Re1 62 Kg2 Rd1 63 h7 Kxh7 ½-½

Hit Back

The inevitable might never happen if you try to have a part in your fate.

☐ **M.Petursson** ■ **A.Lagunow**

Bern 1996

Of the two kings White's is clearly the more vulnerable, with little cover and both g1 and g2 under fire. A natural reaction to the build-up of pressure (Black's queen has just arrived on h3) would be something like 25 Rf3, perhaps. Then 25...Qg4 26 Bg3 h5 and 25...Qh4 26 Bg3 Rdg8 continue to turn the screw. Consequently White sets in motion a counter that uses his trump cards – the advanced centre pawns.

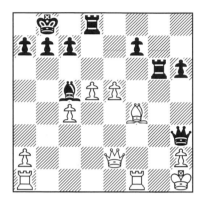

Diagram 17	**Diagram 18**
Position after 24...Qh3	Position after 27...Kc8

25 Rad1! Rdg8

As expected Black doubles, homing in on g1 and g2.

26 d6!

This aims to put Black's king in the firing line, too.

26...Rg2 27 dxc7+ Kc8 (Diagram 18)

Black doesn't want to voluntarily open the h2-b8 diagonal, e.g. 27...Kxc7 28 e6+ Kc8 29 exf7 etc.

28 Qe4

White's strategy works out fine in the game, but Crafty found the following possibility: 28 Rd8+ Kxc7 (...Rxd8 is impossible as the rook on g2 then drops) 29 e6+ Kb6 (29...Kxd8 30 Qd1+) and now instead of one commentator's 30 Rb1+? Ka6 there is the crafty (if you will) 30 Rd6+! Bxd6 31 c5+ **(Diagram 19)**

Not surprisingly such a position is difficult to get to grips with well in advance, especially with today's time controls severely limiting thinking time. 31...Kxc5 (31...Bxc5?? 32 Rb1+ with a quick mate) 32 Rc1+ Kb6 33 Rb1+ Kc7 34 Rxb7+! Kxb7 35 Qb5+ Kc7 36 Qc5+ Kb7 37 Qb5+

and White's double rook sacrifice forces perpetual check.

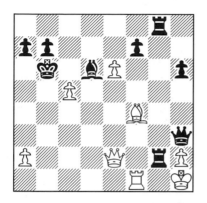

Diagram 19
Position after 31 c5+

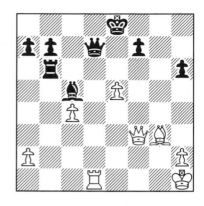

Diagram 20
Position after 34 Rd1

28...R2g6

The deadly threat is ...Qxf1+! followed by ...Rg1+ and mate.

29 Rd8+

An alternative is 29 Rfe1, e.g. 29...Qg4 (threatening ...Qg1+ or ...Qxd1 with trouble for White on the back rank) 30 Rd8+ Rxd8 31 cxd8Q+ Kxd8 32 Qd5+ Ke8 33 Bg3.

29...Rxd8

At this level we would be surprised to see 29...Kxc7? 30 e6+ when Black gets mated, e.g. 30...Kb6 31 Qb1+! or 30...Kxd8 31 Qd5+ Ke7 32 Qd7+, although these things do happen occasionally, thus adding a bit extra to this kind of active defence.

30 cxd8Q+ Kxd8 31 Rb1

An exchange of rooks has effectively taken the sting out of Black's menacing stance, and White's reasonably well placed pieces plus Black's worsened king position make up for the original worries.

31...Qd7 32 Qf3 Ke8!

Now Rd1 wouldn't even threaten Rxd7 in view of the subsequent ...Rg1 mate, something White's next addresses by closing out the g-file.

33 Bg3 Rb6 34 Rd1 ½-½ (Diagram 20)

Any claim Black might have had for an advantage has now gone as there is no longer anything happening on the kingside. After something like 34...Qc6 35 Qd5 Rb2 36 Bh4 Be7 the ending is level.

Alexei Shirov crops up more than once in these pages. Occasionally he is so 'imaginative' in his aggressive play that he comes undone, but his style is such that he doesn't need an invitation to launch a counter when under pressure.

☐ **B.Gelfand** ■ **A.Shirov**

Linares 1997

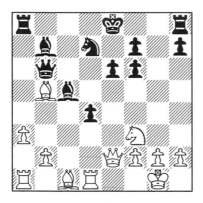 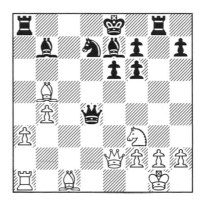

Diagram 21	**Diagram 22**
Position after 17 Bxb5	Position after 19...Qxd4!!

The point scores are even but other factors are in White's favour. Black's king is in the centre and looks like having to stay there as the kingside pawns have been broken and, apart from d4, there are no queenside pawns left. Furthermore, White has two connected passed pawns that bode well for the future. Clearly Black must get busy, as is demonstrated in the following line: 17...Ke7 18 Bxd7! Kxd7 19 b4 Bxf3 and White has a pleasant choice between 20 bxc5 Bxe2 21 Rxd4+ Kc6 22 cxb6 and 20 Qxf3 Be7 21 Bb2 e5 22 Qd5+ Qd6 23 Qxf7 Rag8, with a comfortable lead in both cases.

17...Rg8

Obvious and best. Black decides that the combined pressure of the newly activated rook and the light-squared bishop goes some way to compensating for the pin and the inevitable attack on the d4-pawn.

18 b4

Another natural move, but Shirov prefers 18 Bf4 e5 19 Bg3, e.g.
19...Be7 (19...0-0-0 20 b4 Bd6 21 a4) 20 Re1 0-0-0 (20...Ba6 21 Nxd4) 21
Rac1+ Kb8, when he assesses the position after 22 Nxd4 Qxd4 23 Red1
Qa7 24 Bxd7 Bxg2 25 Bc6 Rxd1+ 26 Qxd1 Bxc6 27 Rxc6 as clearly better for White.

18...Be7

In the event of 18...Bxb4 19 Rb1 Black walks into trouble on the b-file
thanks to the discovered attack (once the bishop retreats) created by
Bxd7+.

19 Rxd4?

This is exactly what Black has been waiting for. Again 19 Bf4! e5 20
Bg3 is the better, more sober treatment of the position, e.g. 20...Bc6 21
Bxc6 Qxc6 22 Re1! Qe6 23 Qe4 hitting both a8 and h7. A well developed
sense of danger is one of the qualities that separates top players from
the rest, but sometimes it is possible that the alarm bells don't ring, in
which case these GMs are less likely to analyse the kind of dangerous
looking line that lesser players would be worrying about, in turn caus-
ing them to miss things that a club player might have under control
because he has to mechanically keep watch for trouble (as opposed to
the top GMs natural warning system). This is akin to a top snooker or
pool player, for instance, missing an easy shot because his mind has
already raced ahead to a later situation in the game, while a one-shot-
at-a-time plodder such as myself will give each shot maximum attention.

 **WARNING: Don't let over-confidence lead to under-
estimating your opponent's dangerous attacking possibilities.**

19...Qxd4!! (Diagram 22)

The '!!' is Shirov's, but I'm sure half of you had already seen this coming. Well done, but did you have this in mind as early as ...Rg8, and
have you worked out what happens after 20 Nxd4 Bxg2 21 Bc6? (we'll
get to that shortly). 19...Rxg2+ is the alternative, but one which allows
White to emerge with a decisive lead: 20 Kf1! (20 Kxg2 Qxd4) 20...Rd8
21 Be3 (21 Rxd7?? Rxf2+; 21 Bxd7+ Rxd7 22 Rxd7 Ba6) 21...Bxf3 22
Qxf3 Rxf2+ (22...Rg8 23 a4) 23 Kxf2 Qxb5 24 Rg1 etc. Neither 20...Bxf3
21 Bxd7+ Kd8 22 Qd3 e5 (22...Bd5 23 Bxe6) 23 Bg4+ Qxd4 24 Qxd4+
exd4 25 Bxf3 nor 20...Bd6 21 Rxd6 Qxd6 22 Kxg2 Qd4 23 Qd3 changes

the picture.

The text is much better because the coming threat of discovered check guarantees either a draw by perpetual or a return of the material from White if Gelfand isn't satisfied with sharing the point.

20 Nxd4 Bxg2 21 Qe3!

After 21 Bc6? Bf3+ 22 Kf1 Bxe2+ 23 Kxe2 White is an exchange down but the connected passed pawns could be a problem for Black. More interesting is 21...Bxc6+! 22 Kf1 Bg2+ 23 Ke1 Bxb4+ (Diagram 23)

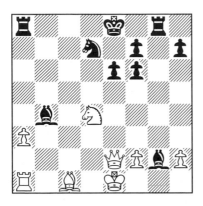

Diagram 23
Position after 21 Qe3!

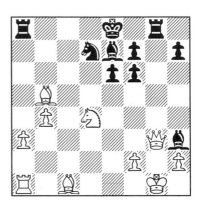

Diagram 24
Position after 24 Qg3

This position is more in keeping with the Shirov approach. Now 24 Kd1 Bd5 25 Qd3 Rg1+ 26 Kc2 Rc8+ 27 Kb2 Bc3+ 28 Qxc3 Rxc3 29 Kxc3 Rf1 is bad news for White. In reply to 24 Bd2 Bd5 25 Kf1 Black can repeat with 25...Bg2+ or try 25...Rxa3 26 Rxa3 Bxa3 27 Qa6 Rg4 28 Qxa3 (28 Nxe6?? Bc4+) 28...Rxd4 etc. Instead of all this White prefers to part with the queen (and on his own terms), after which the struggle continues.

21...Bh3+ 22 Kh1 Bg2+ 23 Kg1 Bh3+ 24 Qg3 (Diagram 24)

This seems to turn down the draw at the cost of a pawn, but Gelfand is able to maintain the pressure, leaving Shirov still with the task of finding good defensive moves.

24...Rxg3+ 25 hxg3 Bxb4 26 Bb2 Bc5!

26...Bd6? 27 Rd1 is one to avoid due to the heat on the d-file. It is important for Black to adjust to the new texture of the game now, as he is under a more subtle kind of pressure. It would be easy to relax and fail to notice a hidden, dangerous feature of the position, for instance.

27 a4

White's trump card advances.

27...e5

Played with the protection of the knight in mind by giving the light-squared bishop a useful role.

28 Nc6! (Diagram 25)

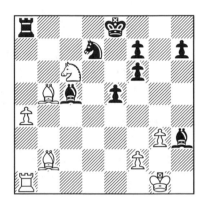

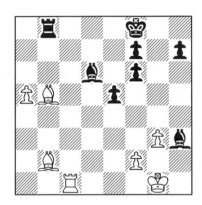

Diagram 25
Position after 28 Nc6!

Diagram 26
Position after 31...Rxb8

Stronger than 28 Nb3 Bd6 because the knight is more of a nuisance on c6. Black's extra pawn is irrelevant and he must neutralise White's queenside lead somehow.

28...Kf8!

Black prepares a nifty defence that requires the knight to be unpinned.

29 a5 Nb8 30 Rc1 Bd6!

Circumspect play from Shirov. 30...Nxc6?! runs the risk of drifting into a difficult ending after 31 Bxc6, e.g. 31...Rb8 32 Bxe5 fxe5 (32...Bxf2+?! 33 Kxf2 fxe5 34 Ra1) 33 Rxc5, or 31...Bxf2+ 32 Kxf2 Rxa5, which could prove uncomfortable for Black.

31 Nxb8

31 Rd1 Bc7 32 Nxb8 (32 Bc3? Bd7) 32...Rxb8 33 a6 Rxb5 34 a7 Ra5 35 Ra1 Rxa7 36 Rxa7 Bd6 comes to the same thing.

31...Rxb8 (Diagram 26) 32 a6 Rxb5 33 a7 Ra5 34 Ra1 Rxa7 35

Rxa7 Kg7

Black is nice and compact and a draw could be agreed right here.

36 Kh2 Be6 37 Ra8 Bc5 38 Kg1 h5 39 Bc1 Kg6 40 Rh8 Bg4 41 Kg2 Kg7 42 Rb8 Be6 43 Rb5 Bd4 44 Rb8 ½-½

A nice display from Shirov, while Gelfand did well to generate renewed pressure after the initial fireworks.

Inconvenience

Although elsewhere in this book we see just how effective hoovering off the pieces can be as a defensive ploy, many players look at simplification too simplistically, jumping at the chance to exchange pieces without even considering alternatives. Most players on Black's side of our next example would see the symmetry as an incentive to steer the game to an ending, and this in itself is quite logical. However, defending slightly inferior endings can be a long and tortuous journey, especially when up against a patient 'grinder' (Karpov and Andersson spring to mind) who is capable of engineering winning chances from ostensibly irrelevant advantages. Watch how the young Brazilian GM uses his remaining knight to cause maximum inconvenience for his opponent, rather than use it to eliminate a centrally posted bishop.

☐ **I.Sokolov** ■ **G.Vescovi**

Poikovsky 2002

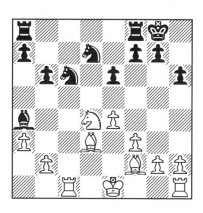

Diagram 27
Position after 20 Nxd4

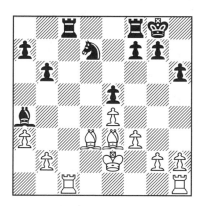

Diagram 28
Position after 23 Ke2

White's bishop pair offers good long-term prospects and might lead the defender to have concerns regarding the dark squares. White also has the more actively posted pieces, while Black's bishop seems out of place on a4. The automatic 20...Nxd4 21 Bxd4 e5 22 Be3 Rac8 looks like a decent challenge but after the simple 23 Ke2 we reach the following position **(Diagram 28)**.

White continues to have a nagging edge, with the superior king and a potentially useful bishop sitting pretty on e3. Meanwhile Black's knight is passive as ...Nc5 leads to a damaging of the queenside pawns after capture(s) forces ...bxc5, leaving White to apply pressure on both flanks. Instead Black finds an annoying (for White) role for his knight.

20...Nc5!

An important intermediate move that avoids an otherwise uncomfortable disadvantage in the endgame.

21 Be2 Nxd4 22 Bxd4 Nb3

Now 23 Rc4?? protects the bishop while hitting Black's in order to avoid discoveries on the d1-a4 diagonal, but this move is as poor as it looks because after 23...b5 24 Rb4 a5 White loses material, 25 Rxa4 bxa4 26 Bc3 being practically decisive, and 25 Rxb3 Bxb3 26 Bxb5? Rfd8 27 Bg1 Rd1+ 28 Kf2 Rc8 embarrassing.

23 Rd1 (Diagram 29)

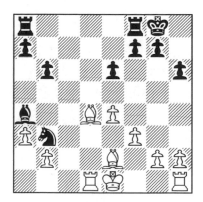

Diagram 29
Position after 23 Rd1

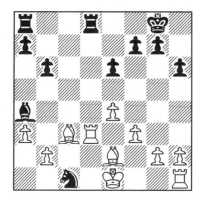

Diagram 30
Position after 26...Nc1

23...Nc5!

The key move. 23...Nxd4 24 Rxd4 is obviously no disaster for Black, but nor is life so simple after Kf2(-e3) and the release of the h1-rook, when

White will maintain control of an important centre file. In fact simple is an appropriate word to describe this kind of situation as White's superiority is plain to see, albeit of a nature that requires persistency in efforts to exploit the advantage, yet a certain mindset to handle Black's lot, too. The text demonstrates that the knight is more than a (short-term) match for the d4-bishop, the location of which is, apparently, part of White's problem.

24 Rc1

White can try to avoid the coming repetition with 24 Rd2 Nb3 25 Rd3, when 25...Rfd8 anyway sees the knight dance on. After 26 Bc3 Nc1 **(Diagram 30)** 27 Rxd8+ Rxd8 the knight even contributes to Black's slight pull, while 26 Be3 Rdc8 27 Bd1 Nc5 leads to easy equality, e.g. 28 Bxc5 Bxd1 29 Kxd1 (29 Bxb6?? Bc2) 29...Rxc5, or 28 Rd2 Bxd1 29 Kxd1 Nb3 30 Rd3 Na5.

24...Nb3 25 Rd1 Nc5 26 Rc1 ½-½

It turns out that not only was Black's bishop actually well placed on a4, but the relationship between this piece and the knight created sufficient activity to render White's conventional advantages meaningless.

The Positional Counter

I have tried to demonstrate with the examples in this book that defending tends to involve nothing special in terms of ideas and strategies. In general, no more is required of us than to look at the salient features of an unfavourable situation and then see how it might be possible to reduce the disadvantage. Here we see how the exchange of a 'bad' bishop for a 'good' one helps shape the defender's game-plan to ultimately take the sting out of White's space advantage.

□ **P.H.Nielsen** ■ **E.Mortensen**

Politiken Cup, Copenhagen 2002

White has a potential target in the shape of the backward d-pawn (hence the knight on f7) and enjoys a territorial advantage in the centre and on the queenside. Black needs to find something constructive else risk being gradually shoved off the board.

14...Bh6!

We are taught that, when in doubt, improve/exchange your worst piece. None of Black's pieces is at all well placed, of course, but, with the e5-pawn fixed and no realistic chance of breaking with either ...d6-d5 or

...f6-f5, the bishop had no prospects stuck away on g7. Nor is it likely that White will launch a kingside offensive, so the bishop won't be required to protect the king.

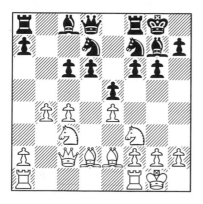

Diagram 31
Position after 14 b4

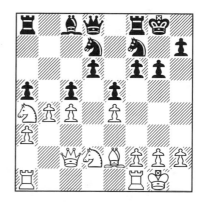

Diagram 32
Position after 17...c5!

15 a3

White is hardly going to play Be1 so must face facts and accept that his flexible bishop will have to go. The point of the text is to concentrate on his queenside lead and wait for Black to make the bishop trade, when the knight can recapture and head closer to the intended action area. However, 15 Bxh6!? Nxh6 16 Rfd1 Nf7 is also possible, when White can try 17 c5!? dxc5 18 bxc5 Qc7 19 Na4 Re8 20 Bc4 Nf8 21 Bxf7+ Qxf7 22 Rd6 with a slight edge according to Mortensen. White prefers to maintain the tension rather than commit the pawns, a decision that he might soon regret.

15...a5!

Remember that Black's bishop was doing nothing whereas White's was about to make a major contribution to the game, so that the coming trade is going to harm White more than Black in terms of influence on the dark squares. With this in mind Black gets to work on the queenside dark squares immediately before White is able to stamp his authority there. In fact the rest of the game sees Black solve his problems by concentrating exclusively on the same colour complex.

16 Na4

In the event of 16 b5 Black has either 16...Bb7 to keep his options open regarding a possible outpost on c5 or seek to close out the game with 16...c5!?, e.g. 17 Na4 Bxd2 18 Nxd2 Nb6, when White has a passed pawn that might not get too far. Meanwhile Black's other knight threatens to undergo a transformation with ...Ng5-e6-d4.

16...Bxd2 17 Nxd2 c5! (Diagram 32)

The theme continues with another assault on the dark squares that can't have been easy to actually play because the pawn was keeping guard over both b5 and d5.

18 bxc5

18 b5 Nb6 leads back to the note to White's 16th move.

18...Nxc5 19 Rfd1

19 Nxc5 dxc5 doesn't help White, an important point being that Black could – if he so wished – eliminate the enemy knight with his bishop should it arrive on d5, whereas White doesn't have this option. Instead White opts to keep the pawn on d6.

19...Qc7

19...Nxa4 20 Qxa4 Qc7 is another possibility, but Black is willing to leave the knights in play. Note that the text removes the queen from the firing line but lays Black open to harassment from a knight on b5 or d5. Some players might see such possibilities as sufficiently inconvenient to put them off ...Qc7, but the queen will have to leave the d-file at some point, so it is better to get on with it now so that other matters can be addressed.

20 Nc3 Ng5!

Black ignores the holes on b5 and d5, which have been a necessary price to pay for the quest to establish a level footing.

21 Nb3 Nge6! 22 Nb5 (Diagram 33)

White has finally managed to hit the d6-pawn but Black's forces are working well together now, although there is still a chance to spoil all the hard work that began with 14...Bh6 should Black not properly analyse the trappy 22...Qe7? 23 Rxd6 Nxb3 24 Qxb3 Nd4? 25 Nxd4! Qxd6 26 c5+ (Diagram 34) Whoops.

 WARNING: If you rely on a tactic you must watch out for nasty (discovered) checks!

The text – which Black must have worked out considerably earlier – both hits and the e4-pawn and sets up a pin on the b-file.

22...Qb7! 23 Nxc5

23 Bf3 a4 24 Nxc5 dxc5 25 Rab1 Qe7 is fine for Black, while 23 f3 further weakens White on the dark squares and doesn't help the bishop, 23...Nxb3 24 Qxb3 Ra6 being about level.

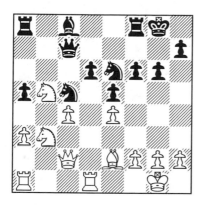

Diagram 33
Position after 22 Nb5

Diagram 34
Position after 26 c5+

23...dxc5

Any hopes of an advantage for White have been dashed by Black's dark-square campaign.

24 Bg4

24 Rab1 lines up against the queen again but after, for example, 24...Qf7 followed by the inevitable ...Nd4 Black is doing well.

24...Nd4 25 Bxc8 Raxc8 26 Nxd4 ½-½

Black could play on here, so perhaps the difference of 175 Elo points had something to do with the decision. Nevertheless, his strategy from the moment we joined the game until the very end successfully transformed what could have been a poor position to a perfectly decent one.

Distraction

With Black it is not unusual to find ourselves short of space across the board, leaving the opposition a choice as to where to attack. More often than not our king comes under fire and, unfortunately, we are obliged to allow enemy forces access to our king's defences. In such circumstances it is imperative to look for distraction elsewhere.

This is exactly what Michael Adams succeeds in doing in the following example. The distraction doesn't necessarily have to force the desired result, rather cause sufficient annoyance or disharmony for the opposition to be knocked off course.

☐ F.Vallejo Pons ■ M.Adams

Linares 2002

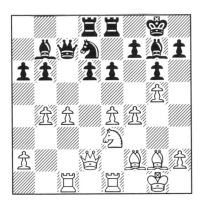

Diagram 35
Position after 23 Ne3

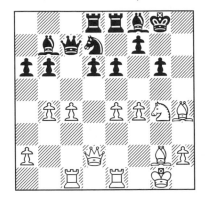

Diagram 36
Position after 26 Bh4

White enjoys a territorial lead on the queenside, in the centre and, in particular, on the kingside. Of course this Maroczy/Hedgehog set-up affords Black a 'coiled' stance with some flexibility regarding pawn breaks, so those players who employ such systems with Black tend to be prepared to operate in cramped conditions.

 NOTE: Being short of space doesn't have to mean being short of resources.

23...h5?!

Stohl goes as far as giving this a '?' in view of the coming infiltration. Instead he prefers 23...f5!?, which does appear preferable. Then after 24 gxf6 Nxf6 25 Qd3 Nh5 we have a typical example of White's multiple pawn advances being undermined, while 24 Qd3 fxe4 25 Bxe4 Bxe4 26 Qxe4 a5! sees Black produce an effective queenside counter, the point being that the usually standard 27 a3? runs into 27...Bb2 etc. This leaves 24 exf5 gxf5 25 Red1 Nf8 with a fine position for Black. The text invites White to engineer a way in on the dark squares.

24 gxh6 Bxh6 25 Ng4 Bf8

Anticipating the attack on the rook, Black offers protection to the d-pawn, as the automatic 25...Bg7 gives White a clear advantage after 26 Bh4 Rc8 27 Red1.

26 Bh4 (Diagram 36) 26...Rc8

Adams avoids the bishop trade despite White's plan, neither 26...Be7 27 Bxe7 Rxe7 28 Red1 f5 29 Nf2 nor 29 e5!? dxe5 30 Nxe5 Bxg2 31 Kxg2 helping Black's cause.

27 Bg5 a5

It is imperative that Black rustle something up on the queenside.

28 a3

Obviously White doesn't wish to break his pawns up and in so doing hand over the c5-square.

28...axb4 29 axb4 Ba6 30 f5 (Diagram 37)

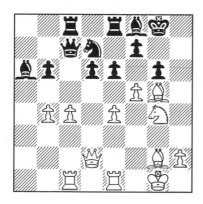

Diagram 37	**Diagram 38**
Position after 30 f5	Position after 31...Ne5!

It should come as no surprise that White is eager to tighten the screw with this advance. Now 30...exf5 31 exf5 gxf5? 32 Nf6+ Nxf6 33 Bxf6 spells the end for Black, while the lesser evil 31...Rxe1+ 32 Qxe1 Bxc4 33 fxg6 is great for White.

30...Bxc4 31 f6

Closing in on the king and effectively ruling out a standard defence. The arrival of the pawn on f6 adds weight to Nh6+ and introduces the transfer of the queen to the kingside with Qf2-h4 which, while not direct, is nonetheless dangerous.

31...Ne5! (Diagram 38)

Black exploits the fact that White is set on a specific course to provide the knight with an influential outpost from where c4 is supported and d3 and f3 come into focus.

32 Nh6+ Bxh6

Allowing White's bishop to plant itself on g7 – the most menacing square on the board under the circumstances – looks suicidal, but the alternative is to invite the queen to the h-file, e.g. 32...Kh7 33 Qf4 Nd3 34 Qh4 Nxe1 35 Nxf7+ Kg8 36 Qh8+ Kxf7 37 Qh7+ etc.

33 Bxh6 (Diagram 39)

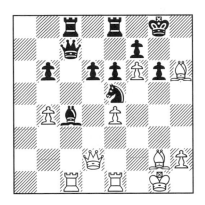

Diagram 39
Position after 33 Bxh6

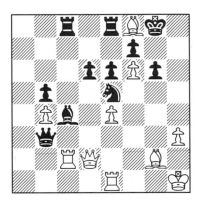

Diagram 40
Position after 37 Bf8!?

This must be exactly what White was planning when he started to apply maximum pressure. Black's king has only a couple of pawns for company, with the rest of his forces denied access. White threatens to lodge the unwelcome visitor on g7 and then send in the queen to h6 with mate on h8. Meanwhile, Black's bishop is pinned to the queen, which appears too far from the action zone on c7. Adams addresses both these problems with his next, strong move.

33...b5!

Now Black need no longer worry about the bishop, and an opportunity presents itself for the queen.

34 Bg7

Of course this is the obvious, direct, powerful looking continuation of White's offensive, but 34 h3 makes sense, e.g. 34...Qa7+ 35 Kh1 Qa2 36 Rc2 Qb3 37 Bf8!? **(Diagram 40)** The point behind choosing f8 instead of g7 is that after 37...g5 White captures with check, thus saving a tempo.

WARNING: Watch out for 'kamikaze' clearance moves that decisively speed up the opposition's attack.

34...Qb6+ 35 Kh1 Ng4 (Diagram 41)

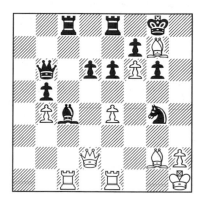

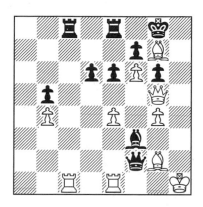

Diagram 41	Diagram 42
Position after 35...Ng4	Position after 38...Bf3

Activating both the queen and knight has given Black a lifeline thanks to the check on f2. Now, try to put yourself in White's shoes, with the seconds slipping by as the time-control approaches, and what is a sensible looking response to the threat to force White's king on to the g1-a7 diagonal?

36 h3?

This is a perfectly natural reaction, the nudge providing the king with a safe haven on h2 and hitting the night for good measure, eviction taking away from Black the vital protection of h6. However, the less obvious 36 Rc2! is correct, preventing any incursion on f2. Play might continue 36...Bb3 37 Rb2 Bc2 (or 37...Rc2 38 Rxc2 Bxc2 39 h3 Qf2) 38 h3 Qf2 39 Re2 Qh4 40 Rxc2 Rxc2 41 Qxc2 Nxf6 42 Bxf6 Qxf6 when the piece outweighs the two pawns. Stohl continues 43 e5 dxe5 44 Qc3, while 43 Rd2 also looks strong.

36...Qf2! 37 Qg5 Be2!

With the mating net almost closing around the target the changing situation over the last few moves must have been difficult for White to come to terms with. Now 38 Rxe2 Rxc1+ 39 Qxc1 Qxe2 40 hxg4 Qxg4 should be at least 'okay' for Black, e.g. 41 Qh6 Qh5+ 42 Qxh5 gxh5 43 Bf1 Ra8! 44 Bxb5 Rb8 and the onus is on White to defend.

 TIP: Challenging the attacker by offering a trade of queens can be an effective means of gaining a vital tempo. In this case Black's sudden aggression is helped by the fact that White's queen must move away, after which Black is able to send another piece into enemy territory.

38 hxg4 Bf3 (Diagram 42)

The bishop now looks comical on g7 and, in view of Black's presence in front of the hitherto untroubled white king, has changed from being what looked like the game winner to the complete outsider.

39 Bxf3

39 Rg1?? Rxc1 is a disaster as recapture allows immediate mate.

39...Qxf3+ 40 Kh2 Qf2+ 41 Kh1

Or 41 Kh3 Qf3+ 42 Kh4 Qf2+ etc.

41...Qf3+ ½-½

Thematic Distraction

It is often the case that unsettling the opposition by making a stand through a distraction policy requires some level of inspiration or imagination in generating a sufficiently busy scene away from the (potential) problem area. But sometimes general considerations and necessities combine to point us in the right direction because the foundation of the desired counterplay is purely thematic. Our next example is typical, Black's defensive strategy almost textbook in its execution.

☐ **V.Golod** ■ **R.Soffer**

Israeli Team Championship 2002

White has an undisputed lead, with the bishop pair and a space advantage that affords him much more room for manoeuvre and possible expansion across the board. While there is nothing seriously wrong with

Black's development, his share of the board is a meagre one and his forces are rather passively posted. The bishop is closed out of the game by White's advanced centre, one knight supports the pinned knight and the major pieces lack breathing space. 'Unleashing' the rook, for example, with 14...exd5, clears the e-file a little but also opens the c-file for White, who can home in on the c7-pawn which cannot realistically be traded for the d5-pawn as this would leave the d6-pawn isolated and vulnerable. We can conclude, then, that Black can either hope that solidity rather than passivity is the key word here, or seek to undermine White's hold on the game in some way. As it is, if we were to study the opening diagram with a view to opting for the latter course, there is indeed a thematic means available.

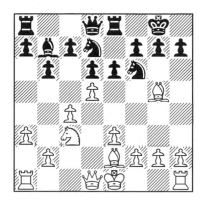

Diagram 43
Position after 14 Be2

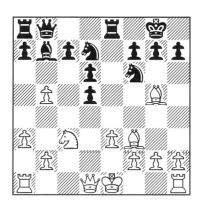

Diagram 44
Position after 16...Qb8!

14...b5!?

This standard 'spoiler' is the kind of counter that, even if you didn't initially see it, you nevertheless appreciate immediately that it appears perfectly natural. The d5-pawn is effectively White's trump card so it makes sense to consider an attack on the supporting c4-pawn. Black is not guaranteed to eliminate White's lead but at least White will be forced to relinquish his hold on the centre. Given that chess often boils down to who can better frustrate the opposition's plans, then this development in itself is already a step in the right direction for Black.

15 cxb5

White should avoid 15 Nxb5?! exd5 16 cxd5 Re5, but 15 dxe6 Rxe6 16 0-0 (16 Nxb5 Bxg2 17 Rg1 Be4 gets White less than nowhere) 16...bxc4

17 Bxc4 Re5 18 Bf4 Re7 seems enough for an edge, although compared with when we joined the game Black has much more freedom.

15...exd5

Now a black pawn stands on d5 and White must weigh up the implications of surrendering his presence there. Note that the c7-d6-d5 set-up is hardly ideal for Black, but the d-pawns do monitor four important squares, while the brief skirmish in the centre has also seen the e-file cleared for Black's rook.

16 Bf3?!

In his annotations to this game Golod points out that he wanted to get rid of the annoying d5-pawn – which is quite understandable – and himself gives the text a '?!' because he believes 16 0-0 h6 17 Bxf6 Nxf6 18 Qd4 to be accurate and sufficient to maintain an edge. This seems to be a reasonable assessment, but with Black's change of pace initiated by 14...b5!? White is bound to focus his attention on the struggle for d5.

16...Qb8! (Diagram 44)

The '!' is Golod's, and I have left it there to help the reader better appreciate how the first move of a good, practical strategy often affords a subsequent logical, desired follow-up additional strength or meaning. At some point Black would have to address the pin on his knight, and b8 even offers the queen an opportunity to make its presence felt now that the distraction has prefaced an opening of the b-file.

17 Bxf6

Giving up the hitherto influential bishop for the hitherto dominated knight must have been a difficult decision to make, but after the automatic 17 0-0 Black responds with 17...Ne4!, when the bishop no longer enjoys its role and Black's knights are transformed.

17...Nxf6 18 0-0

After 18 Nxd5 Nxd5 19 Bxd5 Bxd5 20 Qxd5 Re5 Black is having more fun.

18...a6! (Diagram 45)

And here we have another thematic pawn challenge which fits in nicely with the whole strategy. Many club players who manage to find a promising defensive resource such as 14...b5 become too quickly satisfied with the short-term results and shy away from further activity. An example of this here would be to hold on to the d5-pawn with 18...Re5, but then 19 b4 would make life awkward for Black, for whom ...a7-a6 has become a must with the rook and queen huddled together in the corner. The point is that after 19...a6 20 bxa6 the desired 20...Bxa6? runs into 21 Nxd5 Nxd5 22 Bxd5 Rxd5 23 Qxd5 Bxf1 24 Kxf1 when White is well on top (24...c5?! 25 Rd1 etc.).

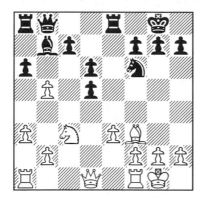

Diagram 45
Position after 18...a6!

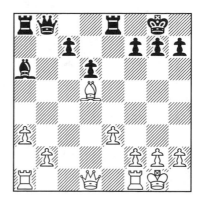

Diagram 46
Position after 21 Bxd5?!

TIP: Go with the flow – don't cut short a thematic course of active defence.

19 bxa6 Bxa6 20 Nxd5 Nxd5 21 Bxd5?! (Diagram 46)

As we will see this 'obvious' recapture requires Black to be on his toes, but 21 Qxd5 is stronger. Black should play 21...Ra7!, when 22 Rfb1 Bb7 23 Qd1 Bxf3 24 Qxf3 c5 followed by ...Rb7 offers some compensation for the pawn as White's queenside is tied down. Then 21...Qxb2? 22 Rfb1 Qc3 23 Qxa8! Rxa8 24 Bxa8 g6 looks good for White after 25 a4, Golod finding the further 25...c5 26 a5 Bd3 27 Rc1 Qb2 28 g3! followed by Bg2-f1 as evidence to suggest 20 Qxd5 is indeed more accurate.

21...Ra7!

21...Qxb2?? sets a trap but allows White a decisive lead. The trap is 22 Qf3 Bxf1 23 Bxf7+?? (23 Rxf1 Qxa3 24 Qxf7+ Kh8 25 Bxa8 Rxa8 26 Qxc7 leaves White a pawn to the good) 23...Kh8 24 Bxe8 Bc4!, e.g. 25 Qf8+ Bg8 26 Rd1 Qe5 etc. The decisive lead results from 22 Rb1!, e.g. 22...Qe5 (22...Qxa3 23 Bxa8 Rxa8 [23...Bxf1? 24 Bc6] 24 Ra1 Qc5 25 Qf3 d5 26 Rfd1 c6 27 e4 is a lesser evil, albeit futile) 23 Bxa8 Rxa8 (23...Bxf1? 24 Bc6) 24 Qa4.

22 Qf3 c5! (Diagram 47)

22...Rf8? is by no means solid as 23 Rfd1! leaves White a clear pawn up in view of the following lines: 23...Qxb2 24 Rab1 Qxa3?? (24...Qf6 is forced, after which 25 Qxf6 gxf6 looks too ugly for Black, while 24...Qe5?? 25 Qxf7+ Rxf7 26 Rb8+ forces mate) 25 Qxf7+ **(Diagram 48)**.

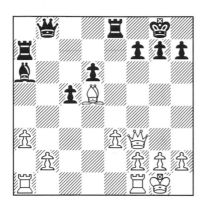

Diagram 47	**Diagram 48**
Position after 22...c5!	Position after 25 Qxf7+

Perhaps this position flashed across White's mind when he recaptured with the bishop on d5. I assume that Black saw this possibility, too, which is why with ...c7-c5 he made sense of ...Ra7.

23 Rfd1 ½-½

23 Rfb1 Bd3 24 Rd1 Qxb2 25 Ra2 Qc3 seems to favour Black, whose c-pawn looks menacing. After (23 Rfd1) 23...Qxb2 24 Rab1 Qe5 the points score is level and Black is fine, which would certainly not be the case after 24...Qxa3?? 25 Ra1, e.g. 25...Be2 (25...Qb2 26 Rxa6) 26 Rxa3 Bxf3 27 Rxa7 Bxd1 28 Bxf7+ Kf8 29 Bxe8 Kxe8 30 Rxg7 etc.

The Positional Pawn Break

Even by being properly aware of the effectiveness when under mounting pressure of exerting a little of our own away from the action area we gain in confidence. And this confidence in turn helps make the game easier to play. Moreover, most players in an attacking role tend only to check out dangerous looking counter-strikes and general tactics rather than ostensibly irrelevant pawn breaks on the other side of the board or positionally oriented 'slow' moves there.

□ **I.Smirin** ■ **B.Avrukh**

Israeli Team Championship 2002

With the centre and queenside looking reasonably stable we are left with White's forces gathered menacingly on the kingside. It takes only a second to spot that f5 is the key square, with White having three pieces and two pawns trained on it! Clearly, the texture of the game will alter when a knight jumps into f5. Note also how White's bishop plays a role on the a2-g8 diagonal. Black, to move, must first consider the most obvious looking threat, namely g4-g5 followed by Nhf5, h3-h4-h5 etc.

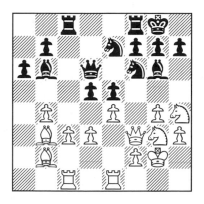

Diagram 49
Position after 23 Kg2

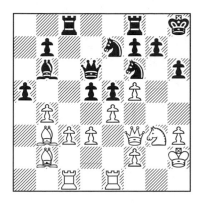

Diagram 50
Position after 26...a5!

23...h6!

Chess authors (myself included) warn their readers about how pawn moves – particularly in front of the castled king – can create weaknesses and/or targets, advice which can serve to dissuade less experienced players from taking sound or even necessary defensive precautions. Here it might seem illogical to bring possible hand-to-hand combat a rank closer, but the immediate prevention of g4-g5 takes priority, and Black judges that the tempo invested soon affords him time to create a distraction.

24 Kh2

Apparently White didn't like the look of the immediate in view of 24 Nhf5 Bxf5 25 exf5 d4! followed by sending a knight to f4 (with check) via d5.

24...Kh8

Black, too, decides that the h-file is a better location for the king.

25 Nhf5

This is the move both players have been waiting for.

25...Bxf5

Obviously Black doesn't want to see his bishop closed out of the game after 25...Nxf5 26 gxf5 Bh7 – it might help protect the king but nonetheless would be cut off from the rest of the game.

26 gxf5 a5! (Diagram 50)

Such a well-timed counter should eventually become second nature.

27 Rb1

27 bxa5 Bxa5 brings the c3-pawn into view, although I prefer that for White to what happens in the game.

27...dxe4

While the text increases the scope of the b3-bishop, this and the following pawn trade opens up avenues and entry points for Black.

28 dxe4 axb4 29 cxb4 Nc6 30 b5 Nd4

Notice how the switch to the queenside has rendered White's kingside ambitions useless. Moreover, not only has nothing happened on the kingside since 26...a5, but Black seems to be enjoying himself more in the new action zone.

31 Bxd4 Qxd4 32 Kg2 Rc3 ½-½

Black is by no means obliged to agree a draw here. Avrukh offers the following line as a sample continuation: 33 Qe2 Qc5 34 Red1 Kg8 35 Rb2 and White is ready for Bd5 or Rd3 etc. This is a rather simplistic example but an important one nonetheless, as accepting his lot by waiting to defend specifically on the kingside would have led to trouble for Black, whereas looking elsewhere for relief proved quite an effortless solution.

Chapter Two

Simplification

Introduction

Reducing the tension or even beating off an attack through the exchange of pieces (simplification) always seems easier when the top players do it. However, for most club players experiencing pressure against their castled king or severely lacking room for manoeuvre, for example, the emphasis tends to be on short-term relief, and failure to think things through is then likely to make matters worse. For instance, simply offering an exchange of queens when under attack – the usual attempt at a remedy at club level – is usually not enough, especially if the defender has made additional compromises to engineer a trade.

Unless you are really desperate there should be a logical foundation on which simplification is based, practical considerations should be borne in mind and – assuming you have a couple of decent pieces yourself – you mustn't continue to automatically hoover off pieces and pawns if there is a possibility that at some point in the process your forces will be superior to those left in the enemy ranks.

In our opening example Black follows up circumspect exchanges by concentrating on centralisation and monitoring White's queenside majority.

☐ **D.Navara** ■ **A.Rustemov**

Morso 2002

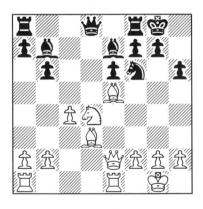

Diagram 1
Position after 17 Qe2

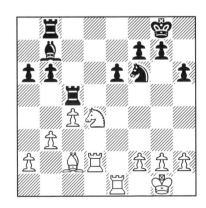

Diagram 2
Position after 23...Rc5

Black's position is okay but White's forces are primed for attack, with a central knight, both bishops pointing at Black's kingside and the queen's rook ready to assume control of the d-file. Not surprisingly Black cannot afford to relax, so before an arrival of the rook on d1 Black opposes the most advanced enemy piece.

17...Bd6

Black can also send his knight on a bishop chasing mission with 17...Nd7 18 Bf4 Nc5 but after 19 Rad1 Nxd3 20 Rxd3 Qc8 21 Rg3 the trade has served only to facilitate White's build-up on the kingside. The text is more direct.

18 Rad1 Bxe5 19 Qxe5 Qb8!

The queen vacates the d-file and practically secures a further exchange because 20 Qe2 Rd8 is fine for Black, as is 20 Qe3 Ng4 (20...Rd8 is possible here, too) 21 Qh3 (21 Qg3 Qxg3 22 hxg3 Rfd8) 21...Qf4 22 Qh4 Rfd8 (22...Qxd4?? 23 Bh7+) 23 Ne2 Qg5.

20 Qxb8 Raxb8 21 Bc2

White wants a clear view of the d-file.

21...Rfc8

At first sight this appears to be an odd choice, but a tempo is gained by hitting the c-pawn and the king is now free to approach the centre.

22 b3 a6 23 Rd2 Rc5 (Diagram 2)

Another far from obvious move which toys with the idea of pushing the e-pawn to dislodge the knight and exert pressure in the centre.

24 Red1 Kf8 25 Bd3 a5 26 a3 Ba6 27 Be2

27 b4?! is tempting (and what Black was drawing attention to when placing his rook on c5) but after 27...axb4 28 axb4 Rc7 29 b5 Bb7 30 f3 Nd7 the changes to the queenside have clearly favoured Black, with both a target on c4 and a fine outpost for the knight on c5. Instead White prepares to switch to the c-file before mobilising his majority.

27...Ne4 28 Rc2 Rbc8 29 f3 Nf6 30 Rdc1 R5c7 (Diagram 3)

With b3-b4 now a genuine possibility Black surrenders a tempo on his own terms. If we compare this position with the one at the start of the example we can see that in terms of avoiding any trouble that might have been looming when we joined the game Black has done very well. In fact thanks to a couple of trades and a bit of shrewd regrouping whatever claim White might have had to an advantage has now gone. White's next is a logical culmination of recent play and White's only try to inconvenience Black.

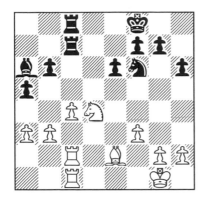

Diagram 3
Position after 30...R5c7

Diagram 4
Position after 41...Kd5

31 b4 Nd7 32 Nb3

32 Kf2 e5 33 Nb3 axb4 34 axb4 Ke7 transposes to the game.

32...axb4 33 axb4 e5 34 Kf2 Ke7 35 c5

A natural follow-up, especially given Black's presence in the centre. White creates a passed pawn but at the cost of a further reduction in forces.

35...Bxe2 36 Kxe2 bxc5 37 Nxc5 Nxc5 38 Rxc5 Rxc5 39 bxc5

As so often happens when one player only has spent most of the game trying to make something of a slight lead, that same player can easily see a series of exchanges as a prelude to a draw – here the offer to trade the final pair of pieces would be eagerly accepted because 39 Rxc5? Rxc5 40 bxc5 Ke6 sees Black mop up the c-pawn.

39...Ke6 40 Ke3 Rc6

After 40...Kd5 41 Rd1+! Kxc5?? 42 Rc1+ the rook is lost.

41 f4 Kd5 (Diagram 4)

White's last was aimed at tempting Black into something like 41...exf4+ 42 Kd4 g5 43 Re1+ Kd7 44 Kd5 when the support of the passed pawn is enough compensation and puts White in the driving seat.

42 Rd1+ Ke6

42...Kxc5 43 fxe5 unnecessarily leaves Black's king on the wrong side of the board.

43 Rc1 Kd5 44 Rd1+ ½-½

Good solid play from Black.

☐ **B.Gelfand** ■ **P.Leko**

Wijk aan Zee 2002

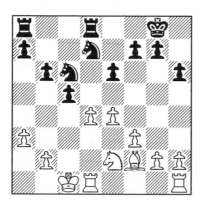

Diagram 5
Position after 19 0-0-0

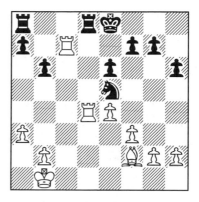

Diagram 6
Position after 24 Rc7

Club players might find this position sufficiently lifeless to agree a draw immediately but White has a slight advantage in the shape of the long-range bishop and the pawn centre. The potentially troublesome prospect of either d4-d5 or d4xc5 is what Black first addresses.

19...cxd4 20 Nxd4 Nde5 21 Kb1

White could settle for the draw now with 21 Nxc6 Nxc6 22 Rxd8+ Rxd8 23 Rd1 Rxd1+ 24 Kxd1 Kf8 but there are practical questions that Black needs to answer.

21...Nxd4 22 Rxd4 Kf8

TIP: Remember that returning the castled king to the centre is a key part of defending once the endgame phase has arrived.

23 Rc1 Ke8

Apparently this was all part of the plan that culminates in the position after Black's 28th move.

24 Rc7 (Diagram 6)

White seems to have made progress since we joined the game, exploiting the central pawn trade by infiltrating on the 7th rank. Indeed the initial edge is now in danger of taking on more worrying proportions unless Black finds an accurate defence.

24...Rdc8 25 Rb7 Rcb8!

Leko voluntarily walks into a pin as the alternative 25...Nc6 loses after 26 Rdd7 Ne5 (or 26...Nd8 27 Re7+ Kf8 28 Rxa7) 27 Re7+ Kf8 28 f4 when f7 falls.

26 Rxb8+

Obviously White shouldn't repeat, especially when the plan looks to be working well thus far.

26...Rxb8 27 Bg3

Despite the removal of a few pieces Black nevertheless remains under pressure, and this time it is White who might gain from an exchange.

27...f6 28 Bxe5

This is the consistent follow-up. It is interesting how easily White can run into trouble here if he becomes a little careless. For example after the aggressive 28 f4 Nc6 29 Rd6 Nd8 Black has been pushed all the way back and White might consider bringing the king into battle with 30 Kc2, but 30...Rc8+ 31 Kd3 allows 31...Nb7 32 Rxe6+? (32 Rd4 is forced, when Black has been helped by f3-f4) 32...Kf7 33 f5 Nc5+, and even 31 Kd2 Nb7 32 Rxe6+ Kf7 33 f5 Nc5 is embarrassing for White in view of the fork on e4 after Rd6.

 NOTE: An ostensibly passive knight can soon switch from defender to attacker thanks to its flexibility.

28...fxe5 (Diagram 7)

No doubt Black had this rook and pawn ending in mind much earlier as he will have had to have taken the structural consequences of the pin into account. White has the more useful looking rook and – more importantly – Black does have doubled isolated pawns, but is this formation as bad as most club players would automatically believe? Leko obviously didn't think so. The advantage of the e-pawns lies in the squares they protect (notably d4 and d5), serving to deny White a way in. Should White seek to remove the e5-pawn by preparing f3-f4, then ...e5xf4 will leave Black's kingside pawns just as healthy as White's.

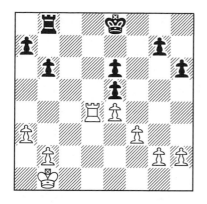

Diagram 7
Position after 28...fxe5

Diagram 8
Position after 33 h4

 WARNING: Don't let stereotypical thinking obscure the evaluation process. Often a key defensive resource will involve some kind of concession that many players would dismiss on general terms.

Let's see how the rest of the game pans out.

29 Rc4 Kd7 30 Kc2 Rc8!

This final part of the simplification process is perhaps the move of the game, Black being prepared to shut up shop against White's more mobile pawns.

31 Rxc8 Kxc8 32 Kd3 Kd7 33 h4 (Diagram 8)

Pawn endings are tricky. With so little to work with we must often walk a thin line, as a mistake at this stage of the game can be disastrous. White's latest seeks to exert pressure on Black's damaged pawns, and Black is faced with a critical choice.

33...g6

The natural, knee-jerk reaction to White's advance is to offer a further trade and clamp down on f4 with 33...g5? but after 34 hxg5 hxg5 White might shift to the kingside with Ke3-f2-g3-g4 etc. With the text Black rules out the restrictive h4-h5 and rather cleverly invites White's next.

34 g3 g5!

Now that g3 is occupied Black can get away with this.

35 Ke3

Of course Black also had to investigate the obvious capture on g5. After 35 hxg5 hxg5 36 Ke3 Ke7 Black holds his ground in the case of either 37 f4 gxf4+ 38 gxf4 Kf6 or 37 Kf2 Kf6 38 Kg2 Kg6 39 Kh3 Kh5 etc. White can also try out the queenside first, but this does not help his cause: 36 Kc4 Kc6 37 a4 a6 38 b4 b5+ 39 axb5+ axb5+ 40 Kd3 Kd6 41 Ke3 Ke7 42 Kf2 Kf6 43 Kg2 Kg6 44 Kh3 Kh5.

35...gxh4 36 gxh4 Ke7 (Diagram 9)

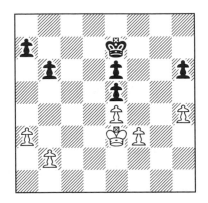

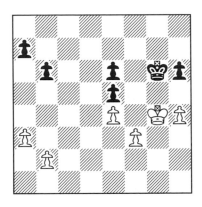

Diagram 9
Position after 36...Ke7

Diagram 10
Position after 41 Kg4

The king has to shadow its opposite number.

37 Kf2 Kf6 38 Kg3 Kg6 39 Kg4 Kg7 40 Kg3

40 f4 exf4 41 Kxf4 Kf6 and there is no way through.

40...Kg6 41 Kg4 ½-½ (Diagram 10)

Black has safely planted the 'Keep Out' sign.

Relieving the Cramp

Simplification to alleviate the pressure in a cramped position is a standard defensive theme. The Maroczy Bind tends to produce precisely this kind of situation, with White enjoying more space across the board.

□ **A.Bokros** ■ **L.Gonda**

Budapest 2002

Black has just played 14...Be6, keeping an eye on the advanced knight and vacating c8 for a rook. White's best is 15 f4 according to Mueller, who gives 15...Nd7 16 b4 with advantage to White. Here the 'automatic' 15...Nc6 hits the queen and protects e7 in order to meet 16 Qe3 with 16...Qa5, but then White has 17 b4! Nxb4? 18 Nxe7+ Kg7 (18...Kh8 19 Qd4+) 19 f5 etc. The text prevents the knight's departure but gives Black an opportunity to simplify.

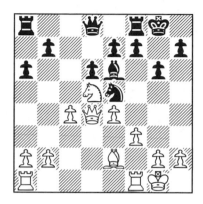

Diagram 11
Position after 14...Be6

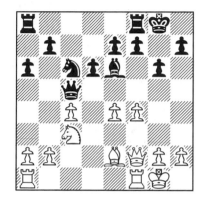

Diagram 12
Position after 17...Qc5

15 Nc3?! Qa5!

Black is not in a position to make threats of his own, e.g. 15...Rc8?! 16 f4 when 16...Nxc4? runs into 17 f5.

16 f4 Nc6

16...Ng4? meets with the strong 17 f5.

17 Qf2 Qc5 (Diagram 12)

The point (of course). There is no denying White's extra share of the board, but in eliminating the most powerful enemy piece Black eases the defensive task considerably.

18 f5

It is true that this thrust abandons the e5-square, but the trade of queens leaves White with hardly anything on the dark squares anyway, so he continues to push forward. As is so often the case in these situations, Black had to look out for post-simplification possibilities: 18 Qxc5 dxc5 19 f5 Bd7 20 Na4? Nd4 21 Nxc5 Nxe2+ 22 Kf2 Bc6 23 Kxe2 b6 and Black emerges in the lead.

TIP: When deciding to simplify, don't stop analysing at the point of the exchange itself.

18...Qxf2+ 19 Rxf2 Bd7 20 Rd1

Introducing the threat of c4-c5 with a pin on the bishop.

20...Rad8 21 Nd5

After 21 f6 exf6 22 Rxd6 Be6 the f2-rook is poorly placed, e.g. 23 Rxd8 Rxd8 24 Nd5 (24 Rxf6 Rd2) 24...f5 25 exf5 Bxf5, or 25...Bxd5 26 cxd5 Rxd5 27 fxg6 hxg6 and the further exchanges have helped Black. In returning the knight to d5 White prepares yet more expansion, but Black remains solid.

21...f6

Finally ruling out f5-f6 for good and adding to the control of e5, just in case. The small price is the hole on e6.

22 b4 Kf7

Protecting e7.

23 b5 Ne5 24 bxa6 bxa6 25 c5

Going for the a-pawn is preferable to the slow 25 Rc1?, when 25...Rc8 sees Black assume the advantage, the e5-outpost now more useful than White's on d5.

25...dxc5 26 Bxa6 Bc6! (Diagram 13)

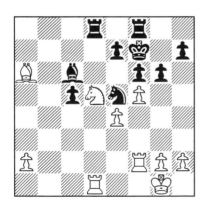

Diagram 13
Position after 26...Bc6!

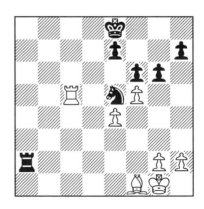

Diagram 14
Position after 31...Rxa2

Once again the bishop prepares to remove the knight, and this time the pressure on the d-file brings about more desired exchanges.

27 Rfd2 Bxd5 28 Rxd5 Rxd5 29 Rxd5 Ra8 30 Bf1 Ke8

Not 30...Rxa2?? 31 Rxe5 fxe5 32 Bc4+, but 30...Ra5!? is possible if Black is looking to test his opponent.

31 Rxc5 Rxa2 (Diagram 14)

With the queenside pawns all gone the simplification is complete, and White now invites a repetition.

32 Rc8+ Kf7 33 Rh8 Kg7 34 Re8 Kf7 35 Rh8 Kg7 36 Re8 Kf7 ½-½

Sometimes exchanging pieces is not necessarily the best option, rather the one with which we feel the most comfortable (or least uncomfortable).

□ **P.Popovic** ■ **Z.Ilincic**

Yugoslav Championship 2002

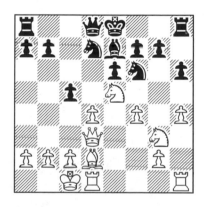

Diagram 15
Position after 13...c5

Diagram 16
Position after 18 Rhf1

14 dxc5 has been proposed as a means to a slight edge, but Popovic has the e6-pawn in his sights.

14 Nxd7 Qxd7

14...Nxd7? 15 d5 exd5 16 Qxd5 is bad for Black.

15 f5!?

White believes his development advantage justifies early aggression, despite having given up the advanced knight. The idea is to exploit Black's uncastled king, e.g. 15...cxd4 16 fxe6 fxe6 (16...Qxe6? 17 Rhe1 Qxa2 [17...Qb6 18 Nf5] 18 Rxe7+ Kxe7 19 Bb4+ and Black is on the ropes) 17 Qg6+ Kf8 18 Rhf1 **(Diagram 16)**.

This would be too much defending!

15...Qxd4! 16 Qe2

Keeping an eye on the e-file while simultaneously giving Black something to think about on the d-file thanks to the discoveries available to the bishop.

16...0-0

The tidy option. Also possible are the almost identical 16...Qa4 17 Kb1 Qg4 18 Qb5+ Kf8 19 Qxb7 Rd8 and 16...Qg4 17 Qb5+ Kf8 18 Qxb7 Rd8, when Black's kingside is again compromised but at least this time it is the black queen which has presence there. However, apart from the fact that this kind of position is not to everyone's taste, it is apparent that it is what White has been looking for, so it is logical to deny White his fun and to try to take the sting out of f4-f5.

17 fxe6

17 Bxh6 Qa4 18 Bg5 Qxa2 helps Black more than White.

17...Qg4 (Diagram 17)

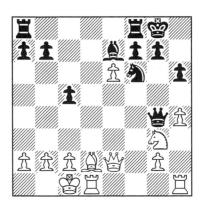

Diagram 17
Position after 17...Qg4

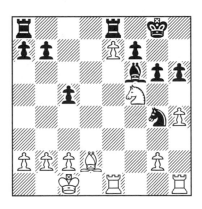

Diagram 18
Position after 21...g6!

Forcing the exchange of queens effectively steers the game to equality. There will be just one loose end to tie up.

18 Qxg4 Nxg4 19 Nf5 Bf6 20 e7

20 exf7+ Rxf7 holds nothing for White (who is then faced with the threat of ...Bxb2+ and ...Rxf5).

20...Rfe8 21 Rde1 g6! (Diagram 18)

Black must address the only potential problem immediately. The greedy 21...h5?, for example, gives White time to secure the e-pawn with 22 Bc3!, when the removal of Black's bishop frees White's knight to come to d6.

22 Nxh6+

22 Nd6 Rxe7 23 Rxe7 Bxe7 24 Nxb7 creates a little imbalance, but one that Black would be happy to see given the state of play on the kingside. Instead White settles for splitting the point.

22...Nxh6 23 Bxh6 Rxe7 24 Rxe7 Bxe7 25 Be3 ½-½

A simple example, but sometimes chess is that simple.

Total Simplification

A useful 'golden rule' is to trade pawns when you're a pawn down. Black manages to gradually clear the whole of the kingside in the following game!

□ **V.Baklan** ■ **A.Riazantsev**

European Championship, Batumi 2002

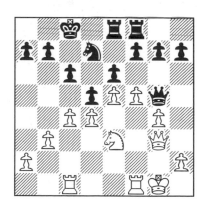

Diagram 19
Position after 21 c4

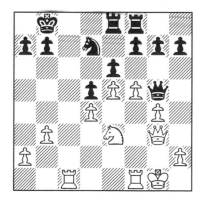

Diagram 20
Position after 22...cxd5

Black is cramped on both sides of the board and White's advance to c4 has brought attention to the c-file with pressure on d5. Lukacs gives 21...Nb6 22 cxd5 exd5 23 b4 as Black's best, with a clear advantage to White, but instead Black escapes the pin.

21...Kb8?

Unfortunately the king now stands on a more dangerous line.

22 cxd5 cxd5 (Diagram 20) 23 Nxd5!

Black must have overlooked that taking on d5 now meets with a nasty discovered check with 24 e6+, which means he must instead continue the game a pawn down. Since his situation was already difficult this seems rather futile, but at least the onus is now on White to convert the material lead.

23...Qd2 (Diagram 21)

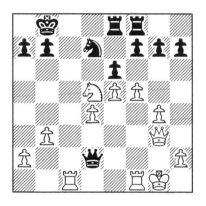

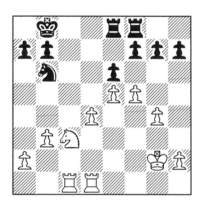

Diagram 21
Position after 23...Qd2

Diagram 22
Position after 27 Kxg2

TIP: Sending the queen into enemy territory is often a good idea when the only alternative is to sit and wait for the situation to further deteriorate.

In this case the mere presence of the queen – hitting a couple of pawns – might succeed in changing White's mind-set from continuing in the same (successful) aggressive mode or consolidating the extra pawn.

24 Rfd1 Qb2

Black prefers to keep an eye on c1 rather than grab the a2-pawn, when 25 Nc7 is strong.

25 Nc3

25 Nc7 spells trouble for Black here, too after 25...Rc8 26 fxe6 fxe6 27 Rb1! but White appears to be settling for the safer approach.

25...Nb6 26 Qg2?!

26 Qd3 is given by Lukacs as promising for White yet the text would be the choice of many players. However, the trade of queens is exactly what Black was hoping for, and we now see an excellent example of systematic liquidation from the talented junior.

26...Qxg2+ 27 Kxg2 (Diagram 22)

White has eliminated his opponent's most dangerous piece to enter an ending in which he has an extra pawn, a useful space advantage and the superior forces...

27...h5!

This thematic challenge is the beginning of the second phase of Black's plan, designed to whittle down the kingside.

28 h3

After 28 gxh5 Rh8 White's once impressive pawn mass is no more, although the extra pawn would nevertheless be significant. White prefers the tidy option.

28...hxg4 29 hxg4 f6!

With one set of pawns gone and another trade coming, Black prepares for further liquidation.

30 fxe6 Rxe6 31 exf6 gxf6 (Diagram 23)

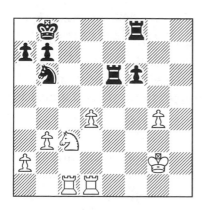

Diagram 23
Position after 31...gxf6

Diagram 24
Position after 37 Kg3

White is still in the driving seat but his lead is now restricted to the (extra) d-pawn as opposed to the intimidating territorial bind seen in the previous diagram.

32 d5

32 Kf3 looks good, simply improving the king.

32...Rd6 33 Rd3?

This natural looking move fits perfectly into Black's game-plan. Instead 33 Kg3! allows White to meet 33...f5 with 34 g5 etc.

33...f5!

Forcing the removal of the kingside pawns (34 g5? Rg8) and easing the defensive task by scaling down the action area to just the queenside.

34 Rf1 Rg6 35 Rf4 Rxg4+ 36 Rxg4 fxg4 37 Kg3 (Diagram 24) 37...Nd7!

A nice touch which exploits the location of White's rook by setting up the fork on e5 in the event of 38 Kxg4?? next. After 37...Rg8 38 Rd4! Black is struggling, e.g. 38...Kc7 39 Nb5+ Kd7 40 Nxa7 Rg5 41 Rb4 Nxd5 (41...Kc7 42 d6+) 42 Rxb7+ Ke6 43 Nb5 etc.

38 Re3 Nf6

Black has achieved – with a little help from his opponent – his goal that was set into motion by the ostensibly aggressive 23...Qd2, namely to steer the game to safer waters through relentless liquidation.

39 Re6 Kc8 40 Re7 Rd8 41 Re5 Kd7 42 Nd1 Re8 43 Rf5 Re1 44 Rxf6 ½-½

Baling Out

Exploiting a material lead to practically force the opponent to trade in his initiative for a level points score is a very useful tactic. Too many players hang on to an extra pawn for too long when defending an awkward position, and by the time they realise it would be prudent to bale out it is often too late.

☐ G.Milos ■ R.Leitao

Sao Paulo 2002

Here we have a fairly standard French set-up in which White concentrates on the kingside and Black on the queenside. The game is well balanced but instead of 17 Qxb4 Rxb4 18 Bxc5 Nxc5 19 b3 with approximate equality White offers a pawn to put his opponent on the back foot.

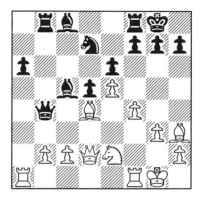

Diagram 25
Position after 16...Qxb4

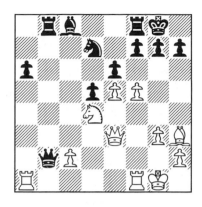

Diagram 26
Position after 19 f5

17 Qe3 Bxd4 18 Nxd4 Qxb2 19 f5 (Diagram 26)

Stepping up the pressure. Black might be a pawn up but the onus is on him to cope on the kingside. Finkel now gives the following variation as an indication of what White had in mind when surrendering the b2-pawn: 19...Nc5? 20 f6 gxf6? 21 exf6 Ne4 22 Rab1! Qxb1 23 Qh6! Nxf6 24 Qg5+ Kh8 25 Qxf6+ Kg8 26 Rxb1 and White wins. 20...Ne4 looks much better, although Black's king is hardly comfortable.

19...exf5 20 Nxf5 Qb6! (Diagram 27)

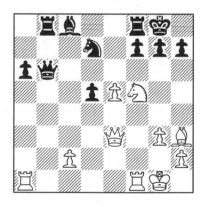

Diagram 27
Position after 20...Qb6!

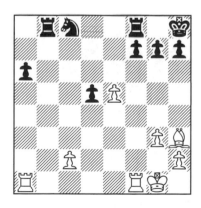

Diagram 28
Position after 23...Nxc8

Both 20...Qxe5 21 Ne7+ Kh8 22 Qxe5 Nxe5 23 Nxc8 Rbxc8 24 Bxc8 Rxc8 25 Rxa6 and 20...Nxe5 21 Ne7+ Kh8 22 Nxc8 Rbxc8 23 Bxc8 Rxc8 24 Rab1 Nc4 25 Rxb2 Nxe3 26 Rxf7 are difficult endings for Black but the text returns the pawn, forces the exchange of queens and – with the help of a well anticipated blockade – steers the game to calmer waters.

21 Ne7+ Kh8 22 Qxb6 Nxb6 23 Nxc8

23 Bxc8 Nxc8 24 Nxd5 Nb6 is nothing special for White, and 24 Nxc8 Rbxc8 25 Rxa6 Kg8 is level.

23...Nxc8 (Diagram 28)

Black has managed to cut across White's plans through a practically forced series of exchanges, happy to restore material balance in view of the resulting pawn configurations. 24 Rxa6 Ne7 seems harmless, so White has one more attempt to sit in the driving seat.

24 e6 f6 25 Rxa6 Ne7 26 Ra7 Rfe8 27 Rd7 Kg8! 28 Ra1 Kf8

White is still on the offensive but has nowhere left to go. The protected passed pawn is securely blockaded and the c2-pawn as vulnerable as d5.

29 Raa7 Rb6 ½-½

In the following game Black sets about systematically simplifying the game with a view to reaching an ending, all the while White's practical chances diminishing with each exchange.

□ **F.Jenni** ■ **B.Golubovic**

Mitropa Cup, Leipzig 2002

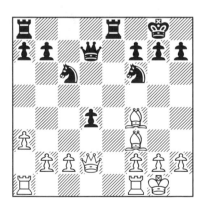

Diagram 29
Position after 17 Bf3

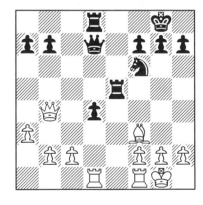

Diagram 30
Position after 20 Qb4

White has the bishop pair and a long-term target in the shape of the isolated d-pawn. Consequently Black cannot wait until the bishops find their range and the d-pawn gets too much attention, so Black wastes no time addressing one of these key factors.

17...Ne5! 18 Bxe5

White lets a bishop go on his own terms, as 18 Be2 Ng6 19 Bd3 Ne4 sees Black get too active.

18...Rxe5 19 Rad1 Rd8 20 Qb4 (Diagram 30)

Black still has a couple of questions to answer. His knight is – for the moment, at least – inferior to the bishop, the d-pawn is under fire and even the threat to b7 needs checking out.

20...a5

As it turns out this fits in okay in the ending, but perhaps better is 20...Re6!?, when 21 Qxb7 Qxb7 22 Bxb7 Rb6 is not what White is looking for, and 21 Bxb7?? Rb8 22 Bc6 Qc8 nets Black a piece.

21 Qc4

21 Qxb7 Qxb7 22 Bxb7 Rb5 followed by ...Rxb2 favours Black.

21...h6!

Simple and useful, investing a tempo to guard against unpleasant back rank surprises.

22 Rfe1 Rxe1+! 23 Rxe1 d3 (Diagram 31)

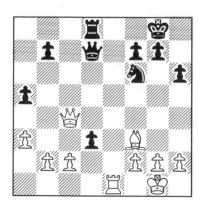

Diagram 31
Position after 23...d3

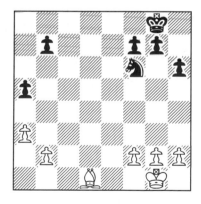

Diagram 32
Position after 27 Bxd1

When we joined the game Black dealt with his opponent's potentially troublesome bishop pair; this time he concentrates on the other main problem and gets rid of the d-pawn. However, he is not out of the woods yet as White has the services of a long-range minor piece.

24 cxd3

24 Rd1? d2 looks too risky for White.

24...Qxd3 25 Qxd3

Given Black's dominance on the d-file it makes no sense for White to avoid the queen trade.

25...Rxd3 26 Rd1

26 Bxb7 Rb3 27 Bf3 Rxb2 and Black has the active rook, while White is yet to give his king some breathing space.

26...Rxd1+ 27 Bxd1 (Diagram 32)

By systematically finding ways to reduce White's accumulated advantages through exchanges, Black has brought about an ending in which careful play should render White's edge (the bishop) irrelevant. The first job is to bring the king to the centre.

27...Kf8 28 Kf1 Ke7 29 Ke2 Kd6 30 Kd3 Nd5

With the king holding a good defensive position Black puts the knight to work.

31 Kd4 Ne7 32 Bb3 f6 33 Bc2 b6 (Diagram 33)

Diagram 33
Position after 33...b6

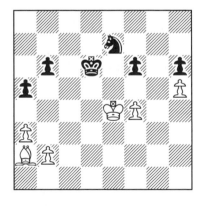

Diagram 34
Position after 46...gxf6

White has the slightly better king and the long-range bishop, but all of Black's pawns stand on dark squares.

34 f4 Kc6 35 g3 Kd6 36 h4 Nc6+ 37 Ke4 Ne7 38 g4

With the entry points all covered White gives the kingside pawns a chance.

38...Ng6

A plain and simple attack on the pawn, perhaps, but forcing the pawn to advance to h5 both reduces White's options and makes for one less possible way in for White's king.

39 h5 Ne7 40 Bd1 Ke6 41 Bb3+ Kd6 42 Bf7 Nc6 43 Bd5 Ne7 44 Ba2 Nc6 45 g5 Ne7 46 gxf6 gxf6 ½-½ (Diagram 34)

White's attempt to make progress has achieved nothing – with no way in, whether or not the g-pawns exist is irrelevant. A nice, easy game from Black, who approached each important feature sensibly and never once gave his opponent anything to bite on. Like other examples in this book, the defensive task revolved around clearly defined but unassuming play.

Chapter Three

The Castled King

- The Unsound Sacrifice
- Have Faith
- Consolidation

Chess would be so much easier if only our opponent had a king. Alas, we must worry about the king's welfare, too, and from the very beginning this is in the forefront of every player's mind. We know from experience and entertaining textbooks that leaving the king in the centre – apart from keeping the rooks apart – can be a dangerous policy. Consequently we follow advice and make sure to castle into 'safety' before it's too late. This conventional way of thinking is conventional because it is in the most part very sound advice, but the geography of the chess board is such that launching an attack against the castled king is relatively easy. Such attacks don't need to be winning to be annoying for the defender, however, so this chapter features a few typical examples illustrate the kind of resources available to both sides.

The Unsound Sacrifice

Despite chess being a game in which good understanding and accurate play are well rewarded, the luck element comes into play when a game starts to get complicated. Some players are luckier than others. These tend to be those who are not afraid to sacrifice pieces in order to unsettle the opposition, after which the opposition often kindly obliges by crumbling at the earliest opportunity, regardless of whether or not there is a successful defence available somewhere. It would be better not to fall into this crumbler category and instead have the confidence to deal with and refute unsound sacrifices...

☐ **P.Popovic** ■ **N.Ostojic**

Yugoslav Championship 2002

In this Caro-Kann position Black has just issued a challenge in the centre with 16...c5. Apart from Black's obvious intention to open lines White needs to think about his advanced knight, the support of which is now being undermined.

17 Ng6?

White's reaction is too ambitious (17 Bf4 Nd5 is better, with an edge for Black, perhaps). However, the onus is nevertheless on Black to avoid the pitfalls that face the defender in these situations.

17...fxg6 18 Qxe6+ Kh8 19 hxg6

19 Qxe7?? Rde8 would be a disastrous follow-up for White.

19...Ng8!

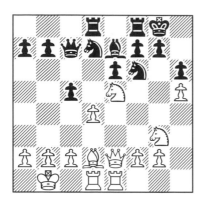

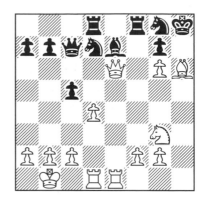

Diagram 1
Position after 16...c5

Diagram 2
Position after 20 Bxh6?

Nice. Most players would play 19...Rde8 here. Then Black has to face 20 Bxh6! gxh6 (20...Bd6 21 Qh3 Rxe1 22 Rxe1, and 22...gxh6 23 Qxh6+ Kg8 24 Rh1 is curtains for Black), e.g. 21 Nf5 Rg8 22 Nxe7 Rg7 23 Qh3 Rexe7 24 Qxh6+ Nh7 (not 24...Kg8 25 Rxe7 Rxe7 26 Rh1 Nh7 27 gxh7+ Kh8 28 Qg6 Qc8 29 dxc5) 25 Rxe7 Rxe7 26 d5 when Black is doing okay but the position might not be to everyone's taste. Lukacs, meanwhile, gives 21 g7+ (! – Lukacs) 21...Kxg7 22 Nf5+ Kh7 (22...Kh8 23 Rh1) 23 Nxe7 Qf4 24 Qe2 with a clear advantage to White. However, I'm not sure what White has after 22...Kg6 – other than 23 Nh4+ etc. Note that 19...Bd6 also runs into 20 Bxh6!, e.g. 20...gxh6 21 Nf5 with problems for Black, or 20...Bxg3 21 Qh3, which is even worse.

20 Bxh6? (Diagram 2)

Although it can be difficult to resist following one sacrifice with another, White should nevertheless settle for 20 Nf5 Rf6 21 Qe4 here, when White has some – if not quite enough – compensation. But the good thing about these tricky, disruptive sacrifices from the aggressive player's point of view is that they present the opposition with more chances to go wrong, which might help explain White's gamble.

20...gxh6!

The gamble would have worked out perfectly had Black played 20...Nxh6? instead: 21 Qxe7 cxd4 22 Rh1! Qf4 23 Ne2 **(Diagram 3)** Black cannot defend against Rxh6+ (...gxh6, Qh7 mate).

This is the kind of 'tactic' Black has to look out for as soon as his king-side comes under pressure. In fact 21...Rxf2 22 Rh1! and 21...Qc6 22

Re6! Qxg2 23 Rh1 show how easy it is for Black's game to suddenly fall apart. Note that the point behind dropping the knight back to g8 was to contribute to the defence of e7 and h6 from the safety of g8, so it makes no sense to then play ...Nxh6.

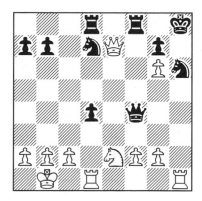

Diagram 3
Position after 23 Ne2

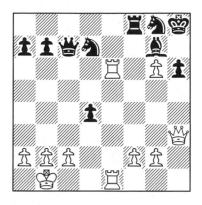

Diagram 4
Position after 25...Bg7

21 Nf5 Rxf5!

Remember that White has already invested two pieces, allowing Black to be practical and return a bit of the booty.

22 Qxf5 Rf8

The three pieces for a rook are enough to bring White's attack to a standstill.

23 Qh3 Bf6 24 Re6 cxd4 25 Rde1 Bg7 (Diagram 4)

The transfer of the bishop to g7 has bolstered Black's kingside and lined up against White's king. It is now a matter of time until Black's larger army makes its presence felt, with the g8-knight, for example, no longer tied down to the defence of h6.

26 Qa3 Rxf2 0-1

White took his chances but was to eventually pay the price when Black proved to be a cool defender. It should come as no surprise that the unsound sacrifice(s) left Black with a few banana skins to avoid (you've been warned).

Obviously it is rather unsettling when the king's defences are first prised open by a sacrifice and subsequently torn apart by another, which is why club players tend to lose so quickly in these circumstances. Better to be optimistic and look ahead to the decisive material lead that will be the deciding factor once the storm is over and the king is safe. Here is a typical example of how a strong player might handle an unsound, albeit tempting, textbook-like double piece sacrifice:

□ **R.Vazquez** ■ **A.Abreu**

Cuban Championship 2002

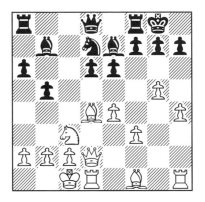
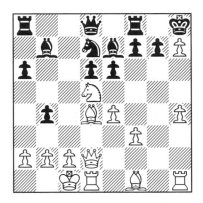

Diagram 5
Position after 13...Bb7

Diagram 6
Position after 16 Nd5?

This opposite sides castling Sicilian is well set up for mutual flank attacks, and White, to move, makes sure he gets in the first blow with a pawn offer designed to disrupt Black's defensive wall.

14 g6!?

White doesn't bother preparing the supporting h4-h5 (met here with ...Bxg5) as either on g6 would be answered by h4-h5, opening lines against Black's king. Black opts instead to ignore the pawn in favour of a queenside counter.

14...b4 15 gxh7+ Kh8

Using an enemy pawn as a shield allows Black to keep the h-file closed so that White must look to the g-file for a target (g7) which Black is confident of holding. Meanwhile, Black is making headway in front of White's king.

16 Nd5? (Diagram 6)

If this were a book about attacking chess we would of course expect to see this sacrifice feature. In fact this is how those who take on the main line Sicilian want to play, Nd5 exd5 being a characteristic of numerous variations. Moreover, it is a key start to many a brilliancy in magazines and 'best' games collections and, as such, is repeated at all levels in the hope of producing similar victories.

16...exd5 17 Bxg7+

The point. One standard Sicilian sacrifice is followed by it's oft seen companion. It is true that Black won't be left with much of a kingside, but the two extra pieces might come in handy, and there is enough of a points lead to hand some back and still emerge from the storm well ahead. The rest of the game revolves around White's attempts to strike while the iron is hot, and Black's endeavours to keep his head above water.

17...Kxg7 18 Rg1+ Kxh7

This time 18...Kh8 is different because Black gives his opponent a chance to make Rg8+ work after, for example, 19 Bh3, although I think Black should hold here, too.

19 Bh3 f5!

Black needs breathing space and is obviously willing to give up an exchange on f5. I say 'obviously' but at club level this is often not the case, and these sacrifices earn more than their fair share of points because the defender for whatever reason hangs on to his booty rather than eliminate the opposition's dangerous pieces.

 WARNING: When defending against a sacrificial attack remember to take your points lead into account if this affords you the opportunity to hold off threats by returning material.

20 Qf4

After 20 Bxf5+ Rxf5 21 exf5 a5 White is reduced to playing only with major pieces, and Black's three pieces for the rook will inevitably decide, e.g. 22 Qg2 Qg8 23 Qg6+ Qxg6 24 fxg6+ Kg7 25 h5 Rh8.

20...Rf6 (Diagram 7)

Perhaps not surprisingly this position has been seen before. B.Muhren-T.Chistiakova, Chalkidiki 2000 continued 21 Bxf5+ Kh8 22 Rg5 Qe8 23 Rdg1 Qf7 24 Qg4 Rxf5! 25 Rxf5 Nf6 26 Qf4 Rg8! 27 Rxg8+ Qxg8 and because 28 Rxf6 runs into 28...Qg1+ 29 Kd2 Qd4+, White played 28 Rg5, when 28...Qh7 was the beginning of the end for White.

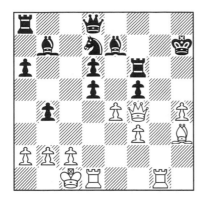

Diagram 7	Diagram 8
Position after 20...Rf6	Position after 23...Kf7

21 Rg5 Qf8 22 Rh5+

22 Bxf5+ Rxf5 23 Rxf5 Nf6 and Black has sufficient defenders.

22...Kg8 23 Bxf5

23 Rg1+ Kf7 24 Rh7+ Ke8 25 Rgg7 is the kind of possibility that would scare many players who, if they managed to see it in advance, might get themselves into serious trouble trying to avoid it. Doubled enemy rooks in the heart of our defences, coupled with threats directed at the king and queen, can indeed create phantoms in the mind of the defender, but in fact after the calm 25...dxe4 26 Rxe7+ Qxe7 27 Rxe7+ Kxe7 Black has two rooks and a knight for a queen and his king is perfectly safe.

 TIP: When the attacker has invested more than a piece the defender should keep an eye out for attempts to win his queen, as such threats or – on the defender's part – ostensibly last-ditch defensive resources tend to result in the attacker paying too high a price.

This is exactly what happens in the game.

23...Kf7 (Diagram 8)

The king heads for the hills.

24 Qg4

24 Bg6+!? Kxg6 25 Qg4+ Kf7 26 Qxd7 cuts off the king's escape route but at the cost of another pair of minor pieces leaving the arena. White remains two pieces down, so that after 26...Bc8 27 Rh7+ Kg8 28 Qxe7 Qxe7 29 Rxe7 dxe4 30 fxe4 Bg4 31 Rg1 Rf4, for example, he has failed to catch up.

24...Ne5!

Good, no-nonsense practical play from Black, who is able to visualise an advantageous way out of the woods.

25 Rh7+ Ke8 26 Qh5+ Kd8! 27 Rh8 Kc7 28 Rxf8 Raxf8 29 Rg1 (Diagram 9)

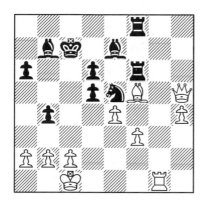
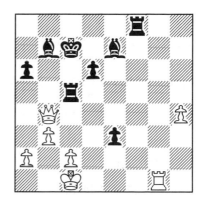

Diagram 9	Diagram 10
Position after 29 Rg1	Position after 34...e3

Let's have a quick look at the score – Black has a rook and two perfectly healthy pieces for the queen. His knight is massive and his king tucked away nicely. In this kind of situation, unless the player with the queen has something to bite on, the larger army tends to be in charge.

29...R6f7!

29...Nxf3? seeks to exploit Black's power on the f-file but is answered by the creation of another pin, 30 Rg7! Kd8 31 Qh7 etc.

30 b3

30 Be6 Rxf3 31 Qh7 Rf1+ 32 Rxf1 Rxf1+ 33 Kd2 Kd8 34 exd5 a5 favours Black but is easier for White to handle than the more accurate 30...Rf4! (threatening to trap the queen) 31 Qh7 Kd8 32 Rg8 dxe4, when White doesn't have the steadying influence of the d5-pawn.

30...Nxf3! 31 Qxf3?

It is only natural to want rid of the knight, but a lesser evil is 31 Rd1 dxe4 32 Be6 Rg7 33 Qa5+ Kb8 34 Bd5, or 32...Ne5!? 33 Bxf7 Rxf7 with three pieces for the queen.

31...dxe4 32 Qe2 Rxf5 33 Qc4+ Rc5 34 Qxb4 e3 (Diagram 10)

After coping well with the initial flurry of activity in front of his king Black brought in the defenders, found a route out of the heat for his king, 'allowed' White a reward for his aggression by giving up his queen and then pointed out the reality of the subsequent situation by mobilising his larger army. A rook, two bishops and an eager passed pawn are simply too much to handle.

35 Rg7

35 Kb1 Rf2 and 35 Qd4 Rf2 36 c4 Rxa2 are equally unpleasant alternatives.

35...Re5 36 Rg1 e2 37 Re1 Bc6 38 Qc4 Rf2 39 Qxa6 Bxh4 40 Qc4 Rh2 0-1

Coping with tricky but ultimately faulty attacks is difficult enough, but dealing with sound tactics is another story altogether.

□ **A.Grischuk** ■ **B.Gelfand**

Wijk aan Zee 2002

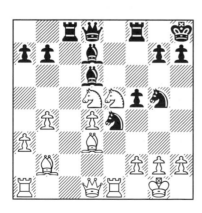

Diagram 11
Position after 18 Ne5

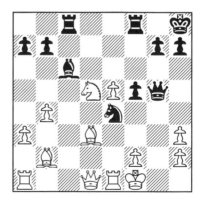

Diagram 12
Position after 21...Bc6!?

White has an extra pawn but – with Black's forces aimed at his king-side – must have been a little bit concerned...

18...Nh3+!

And quite right, too. From here on in White finds himself up against the ropes as his king comes under fire.

19 gxh3 Qg5+ 20 Kf1

20 Ng4 Nxf2! is awful for White.

20...Bxe5

Black has enough fire-power to maintain the momentum so he elimi-nates a potentially useful defender.

21 dxe5 Bc6!? (Diagram 12)

Ftacnik writes that Black's latest 'crowns' the original ...Nh3+, and that White 'has to play with extreme caution' here. Now White can try to tidy up the kingside with 22 f4 Qh6 23 Bxe4 fxe4 24 Kg1 (24 Ne3? Qxf4+ 25 Kg1 Qf2+ 26 Kh1 Qxb2) but after 24...Rcd8 25 Qg4 Rxd5 26 Bc1 Rd3 Black is still having more fun. The natural 22 Ne3 Rcd8 23 Qc2 might be okay, although after the plausible 23...Rxd3 24 Qxd3 Qf4 25 Nd1 Nd2+ 26 Kg1 Nf3+ 27 Kf1 Black has the option of turning down the draw with 27...Qxh2 28 Ke2 Qxh3.

TIP: When under attack, unless you believe you will see more than your opponent it is preferable to keep his op-tions to a minimum.

22 Bc1! Qh4 23 Bxe4 fxe4 24 Be3

This has been a good defensive transfer of the bishop because f2 clearly needed protecting sooner or later. Posting the bishop on e3 has another use, too in that it blockades Black's e-pawn. This is evident in 24 Ra2 e3! 25 Rxe3 Qc4+, which isn't such bad news for White but the opposite coloured bishops mean Black would continue as the aggressor. Then there is 24 Nf4 Rxf4 25 Bxf4 Qxh3+ 26 Kg1 e3 **(Diagram 13)**.

Thanks to Be3 Black's remaining minor piece is denied direct access to the attack, leaving the queen to do the work.

24...Qxh3+

24...Rcd8? 25 Qg4 lets White off the hook.

25 Kg1 Bxd5

25...Rcd8? 26 Nf4 Qh4 27 Ng2 and White is a clear piece up.

26 Qxd5 (Diagram 14)

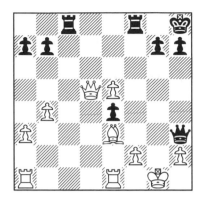

Diagram 13
Position after 26...e3

Diagram 14
Position after 26 Qxd5

 WARNING: Keep an eye on your opponent's quiet pieces – check for (and prevent) ways of them coming to life.

Allowing your opponent to dictate the game is not a good policy, but giving an attacker the opportunity to turn down a draw that you would be content with in favour of a further but faulty winning attempt is often rewarded. In this case Black might be tempted into following up his hitherto hyper-aggressive play with 26...Rc6?, but then White has the unlikely but decisive 27 Bf4!, when capture is impossible in view of the back rank mate, leaving the g-file closed after the subsequent Bg3 etc.

 NOTE: The latter stages of a sacrificial attack might involve making concessions that can be exploited with a surprise resource. Gelfand is not one to miss cheeky features such as Bf4, and instead settles for the perpetual.

26...Qg4+ 27 Kf1 Qh3+ 28 Kg1 Qg4+ 29 Kf1 ½-½

Have Faith

Sometimes we face attacks against our king in which there seem to be too many enemy pieces closing in, but it is surprising how calm, accurate defence can save the day, especially when we have been allowed – even invited – to collect material elsewhere. Here is a good example of a menacing build-up of forces against a cramped king position failing to hit the target despite multiple threats and sacrifices. (Note that a certain amount of technological assistance was required for me to explore the ins and outs of this game, so Black's defensive display is all the more impressive.)

□ E.Bareev ■ A.Morozevich

Cannes 2002

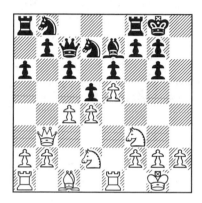

Diagram 15
Position after 12...hxg6

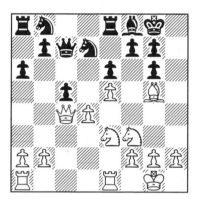

Diagram 16
Position after 16...c5

A trade of bishops on g6 has left Black looking a little vulnerable to attack on the kingside. Consequently, with a space advantage and good control of the centre, White sends his forces to the kingside.

13 Nf1

A temporary retreat that releases the bishop and prepares to relocate the knight to a more aggressive post.

13...Re8 14 Bg5 Bf8

And here we have another positive backward step. Black is averse to exchanging bishops for two reasons – after 14...Bxg5 15 Nxg5 there is the unpleasant threat of swinging the queen over to h3 with h7 under fire, while Black's bishop could well prove to be more useful as a defender than White's as an attacker.

WARNING: When under attack, don't automatically trade pieces in order to alleviate pressure – consider the defensive properties of your pieces.

15 Ne3 dxc4

Black cannot idly sit and wait for the onslaught to gain pace, so he wastes no time generating counterplay on the queenside.

16 Qxc4

White recaptures this way because the queen can easily reroute to the kingside, while the knight is heading for g4.

16...c5 (Diagram 16)

For now the c-pawn is pinned, but this push entertains both a later ...c5xd4 or the space-gaining ...b7-b5 followed by ...c5-c4.

17 Ng4

17 b4 b5 18 Qc3 c4 19 d5 is good for White, but Black can improve with 17...b6 18 bxc5 bxc5 19 Rac1 Nc6 20 Red1 Rec8, when the queenside has opened enough to distract White from the kingside (note how the bishop then looks ineffective on g5).

17...b5 18 Qe2 c4 19 Rac1

Given the combative styles of these players, what follows is hardly surprising, but the text prefaces an unnecessary if complex strategy.

19...Nc6 20 b3?!

With the last few moves in mind it would make more sense to play 20 Ne3. However, White sent the knight to g4 for a reason and the text is the consistent, albeit dubious follow-up.

20...c3 (Diagram 17)

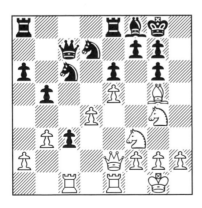

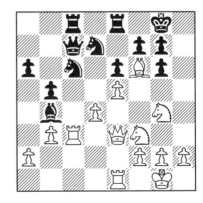

Diagram 17
Position after 20...c3

Diagram 18
Position after 23 Bf6?

21 Qe3

21 Rxc3 Bb4 wins the exchange, although White volunteers the material soon anyway. First he nudges the queen nearer Black's kingside.

21...Rac8

21...b4 is another option to secure the passed pawn, after which Black is doing well. Nevertheless this would effectively slow the game down and therefore give White more time to concentrate on the kingside.

22 Rxc3 Bb4 23 Bf6? (Diagram 18)

White unleashes his weapon and prepares to throw the kitchen sink at the enemy king, rather than make do with 23 Rc2 Bxe1 24 Qxe1 Nb6 25 Qd2 Nd5 26 Ne3. The rest of the game revolves around White's endeavours to bombard Black's king, and Black's efforts to survive the onslaught and effectively emerge from the smoke-filled battleground with fewer casualties. I suspect that both players had anticipated this position and some of the ensuing complications, with Black hoping, in fact, that such an attack would be launched.

TIP: In a cramped but solid position it is often the case that tempting the opponent into a brutal but committal attack by threatening to generate activity of your own is a more promising strategy than passively allowing him to gradually exploit (risk-free) a space advantage.

23...gxf6!

Many players seem to react to a proposed sacrifice by exchanging the offered piece rather than accepting it, on the grounds that this is safer than falling in with the opponent's plans. This is possible here with 23...Nxf6, especially since Black anyway takes a points lead after 24 exf6 Bxc3. The subsequent 25 fxg7 Nxd4 26 Nxd4 Bxe1 27 Qh6 leaves Black with two choices. After 27...f6 White can force a draw with 28 Qxg6 Qxg7 29 Nxf6+ Kf8 30 Nh7+ Kg8 31 Nf6+ Kf8 32 Nh7+, or 28 Qh8+ Kf7 29 Qh7 Bxf2+ 30 Kxf2 Qf4+ 31 Nf3 Rc2+ 32 Kf1 Rc1+ 33 Kf2 Rc2+ etc. Note that 29 g8Q+? Rxg8 30 Qh7+ Rg7 31 Nh6+ Ke7 32 Qxg7+ Kd6 33 Qxf6 backfires after 33...Qc1, e.g. 34 Nf7+ Kc5! 35 Nxe6+ Kb4 **(Diagram 19)**.

Meanwhile, 27...f5 28 Qh8+ Kf7 29 Ne5+ Ke7 (29...Qxe5 30 g8Q+ Rxg8 31 Qxe5) 30 Nxg6+ Kf7 also leads to a draw, whereas attempts by Black to run fail in the event of both 30...Kd6?? 31 g8Q Rxg8 32 Qe5+ Kd7 33 Qxe6+ Kd8 34 Nc6+ and 30...Kd7? 31 Nf8+ Rxf8 32 gxf8N+! (32 gxf8Q Bxf2+ 33 Kxf2 Qf4+ 34 Nf3 Rc2+ 35 Kf1 Qc1+ 36 Ne1 Qf4+)

32...Kd6 (32...Rxf8 33 Qg7+ Kd6 34 Qxc7+ Kxc7 35 Nxe6+) 33 Qh6 Rxf8 34 Qxf8+ Kd5 35 Nf3.

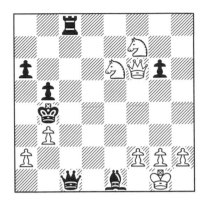

Diagram 19
Position after 35...Kb4

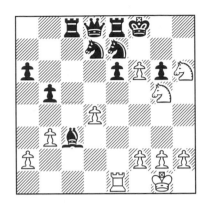

Diagram 20
Position after 29 Ng5

24 exf6 Qd8!

Black correctly judges that the f6-pawn is a key player that must be addressed immediately. The otherwise logical 24...Red8 provides some breathing space for the king (see later) but fails to keep White at bay: 25 Nh6+ Kf8 26 Nxf7 Nxf6 27 Qh6+ Kxf7 (27...Ke7 28 N7g5) and now comes 28 Rxc6!, when 28...Qxc6 29 Ne5+ Ke7 30 Qg7+ Kd6 31 Nxc6 Rd7 32 Qxf6 Bxe1 33 Ne5 works out well for White. Instead 28...Qb7 29 Ng5+ Kg8 30 Rec1! Rxc6 31 Rxc6 sees White exploit the defensive obligation of Black's queen along the seventh rank to invite an endgame after 31...Re8 32 Qxg6+ Qg7 33 Qxg7+ Kxg7 34 f4 which appears to offer enough pawns for the piece.

25 Qg5

25 Nh6+ Kf8 26 Nxf7 scores in the case of 26...Kxf7 27 Ng5+ Kf8 (27...Kg8 28 f7+ Kg7 29 fxe8Q Qxe8 30 Nxe6+ Kg8 31 Qh6 Bf8 32 Qf4) 28 Nxe6+ Kg8 (28...Kf7 29 Qh6) 29 f7+! Kxf7 30 Nxd8+ Rcxd8 31 Qf4+ Nf6 32 Rxe8 Rxe8 33 Re3, but Black has the simple 26...Qxf6. One commentator wrote that 25 Qf4 Bxc3 26 Nh6+ Kf8 27 Qd6+ Ne7 'also gets White nowhere' but 28 Qxe6!! in fact gets White to the end of the rainbow since it leads to forced mate! Meeting the recapture 28...fxe6 with 29 Ng5 **(Diagram 20)** gives us an odd position indeed.

Amazingly, even if Black removes the annoying pawn on f6, then White still delivers mate with 30 Nxe6 as g7 is covered anyway. Ruling out the mate on e6 by, for example, 29...Nf5 walks into another mate on h7. Very nice. Unfortunately for White there is the practical 27...Re7! 28 fxe7+ Qxe7 with an extra piece.

25...Bxc3 (Diagram 21)

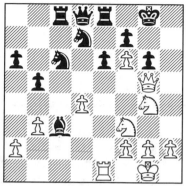

Diagram 21
Position after 25...Bxc3

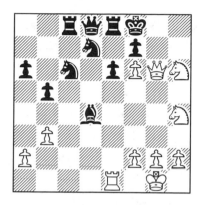

Diagram 22
Position after 28 Qxg6

Despite the gathering enemy forces in front of his king Black pockets the rook.

26 Nh4 Bxd4

26...Bd2 looks a bit flashy but is also good, e.g. 27 f4 (27 Nh6+ Kf8 28 Qxg6 Qxf6; 27 Qxd2 Nxf6) 27...Bc3 28 Nxg6 Bxd4+ 29 Kh1 Bxf6 etc. However, 26...Bxe1? is too greedy and ignores the goings on in the danger zone: 27 Nxg6 Nxf6 28 Nxf6+ Qxf6 29 Qxf6 fxg6 30 Qxg6+ with a perpetual.

27 Nh6+

Black also had to get to grips with the surprisingly complex variation 27 Nxg6 Bxf6 28 Ne7+ (28 Nh6+ Kg7) 28...Kf8 29 Nxf6 Nxf6 30 Nxc8 Nd5 31 Qh6+ Kg8 32 Re4 Nf4!? (simultaneously obstructing the rook while clearing the d-file for the queen) 33 h4 Ng6 34 h5 Nge5 35 Na7!? Qd1+ 36 Kh2 Qg4!.

27...Kf8

27...Kh7 is another option.

28 Qxg6 (Diagram 22)

White has one last – albeit futile – throw of the dice.

28...Bxf2+

A nice way to finish. 28...Qxf6 also wraps up for Black, but 28...fxg6??, allowing immediate mate on g6, would be a surprise at almost any level.

29 Kh1

29 Kxf2 Qxf6+.

29...Qxf6 30 Qg8+ Ke7 0-1

White has finally run out steam.

Consolidation

Finding the defensive wall in front of your castled king suddenly broken doesn't have to be as bad as it looks. If it is possible to anticipate such a disruptive attempt then – unless you can (or wish to) avoid it – measures can be planned to address the matter, while it is by no means unusual to be able to consolidate and nip the opposition's desired follow-up in the bud.

□ **P.Kotsur** ■ **M.Sorokin**

Goodricke International, Calcutta 2002

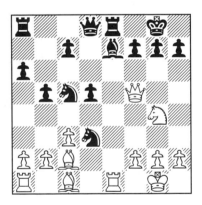

Diagram 23
Position after 17 Ng4

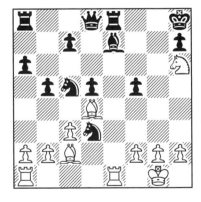

Diagram 24
Position after 22 Bd4+

Black is a pawn up but his knights are busy working overtime to restrict White's menacing light-squared bishop, which has teamed up with the queen to introduce the mating possibility on h7. Unfortunately for Black he can't exploit White's apparent vulnerability on the back rank as after 17...Bd6 18 Rxe8+ Qxe8 19 Bxd3 White will be able to meet the check on e1 with a block on f1.

Given that White seems to be hanging his hopes on the b1-h7 diagonal and that, otherwise, his rook is hanging, you might think that after 17...g6? White comes unstuck or must take a perpetual, but after 18 Nh6+ Kh8 19 Nxf7+ it is Black who is in trouble. In the event of 19...Kg8 (19...Kg7 20 Bh6+ Kg8 21 Qg4 Qd7 22 Qd4 Bf6 23 Qxf6 Rxe1+ 24 Rxe1 Qxf7 25 Qxf7+ Kxf7 26 Rd1 Nxb2 27 Rxd5 Re8 28 Kf1) 20 Nh6+ Kh8 there comes the uncompromising 21 Be3! gxf5 22 Bd4+ **(Diagram 24)**.

This almost looks self-explanatory now, but to have factored the position into deliberations surrounding the initial position is another matter. If you wouldn't fancy Black's chances you'd be absolutely right. After 22...Bf6 23 Rxe8+ Kg7 24 Rxd8 Rxd8 25 Nxf5+ Black runs into b2-b4, embarrassing the knights. Meanwhile 22...Ne5 23 Rxe5! Kg7 24 Nxf5+ is decisive, e.g. 24...Kf8 25 Rxe7 Ne6 (25...Rxe7 26 Bxc5 and the three pieces will overpower the queen) 26 Bf6 and now instead of the greedy 26...Qc8, when 27 Rxh7 threatens the deadly Nh6 followed by mate on f7, Black has to face facts with 26...Rxe7 27 Bxe7+ Qxe7 28 Nxe7 Kxe7 29 Bxh7 when the three connected passed pawns are ready to roll. 24...Kg8 also fails to keep White at bay: 25 Nh6+ Kf8 (25...Kg7 26 Rxe7+ Kxh6 27 Be3+ mates) 26 Rf5+ Bf6 27 Bxf6 Qc8 28 Bd4+ Ke7 29 Bxc5+ and the curtain is coming down on Black. So our start position could in fact prove disastrous for Black if he were to try the plausible looking 17...g6. Instead Sorokin is on the ball.

17...Qc8!

Offering an exchange of queens that White can ill afford due to the pawn deficit, and practically forcing White's next.

18 Bxd3 Nxd3 19 Nh6+!

Black would obviously prefer to see 19 Qxd3 Qxg4 20 Qxd5, when 20...Rad8 is a bit tricky and should be roughly level after 21 Qc6 (21 Rxe7?? Qd1+!) 21...Qg6 22 Qxg6 (22 Qxc7? Bd6) 22...hxg6 etc. The disruptive check on h6 gives Black something to think about. At club level this might prove successful in that Black will be intimidated, while here Sorokin is up to the task.

19...gxh6 20 Qxd3 Bd6 21 Bxh6 (Diagram 25)

Not only has White regained his pawn, but there is the exposed enemy king to further boost his morale. For the moment Black doesn't have to worry about a mate on g7 because White isn't getting to the g-file (of course most players would worry anyway, just in case...) and can therefore concentrate on shoring up his defences.

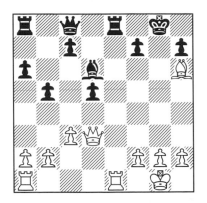

Diagram 25
Position after 21 Bxh6

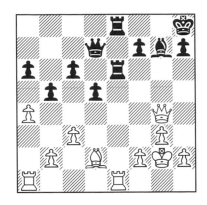

Diagram 26
Position after 27...Bg7

21...Re6!

This is solid as well as stubborn, whereas something like 21...c6?! is solid looking but threatens nothing. Thus White is given time for the annoying 22 Qd4 when the mate threat does arrive and forces 22...Bf8 23 Bxf8, with a big position for White after either 23...Rxe1+ 24 Rxe1 Qxf8 25 Re3 h6 26 Qg4+ Kh8 27 Qd7, or 23...Rxf8 24 Re3 f6 25 Rae1 etc.

> TIP: Given a choice between a couple of candidate solid moves, select the one which causes the opposition the most inconvenience.

22 Bd2

22 Be3 allows White to double rooks while sheltered by the bishop. Then 22...Qd7 23 Re2 (23 Qf5? Bxh2+! and the bishop is immune due to the discovered attack on White's queen after the subsequent check on h6) 23...c6 24 Rae1 Rae8 25 Qf5, and this time 25...Bxh2+ 26 Kxh2 Rh6+ 27 Bxh6 leaves the queen safe thanks to the mate on e8, so 25...f6 is called for, when Black's queen is ready to nip across the rank to help the king, the slightly damaged kingside pawns are fairly safe and the queenside is solid. With the text White opts to leave his rooks where they are in order to perhaps prise open the queenside with a2-a4.

22...Qd7 23 g3

Not 23 Qxd5?? Bxh2+ and the queen goes.

23...c6 24 Qf3 Rae8 25 Qg4+ Kh8 26 Kg2

By creeping forward slightly with g2-g3 and Kg2 White has been able to pin the rook to the queen as ...Rxe1 is no longer check. Additionally, the queen is well placed on g4 because it combines well with Be3-d4+, something which prompts Black's next.

26...Bf8!

 NOTE: Don't forget to check out which piece(s) might be more useful elsewhere.

27 a4 Bg7 (Diagram 26)

Black couldn't have conducted the game any better. He has brought both rooks to the only open file, sent the bishop to both support the king and monitor the long diagonal and solidified the queenside pawn mass. Obviously White has an edge, but this is more cosmetic than realistic.

28 axb5 axb5 29 Be3

White entertains a switch to the a-file.

29...R6e7!

This rook switch offers a trade of queens and keeping an eye on the second rank.

30 Qxd7

Refusing the exchange doesn't improve White's prospects. In fact the game is now heading for the draw that White has been trying to avoid.

30...Rxd7 31 Bd4 Rdd8

Black doesn't want to take on d4 as this would leave the (backward) c6-pawn both fixed and exposed.

32 Kf3 b4 (Diagram 27)

Notice how Black is dealing with each of the weaker elements of his position. Already with an inferior kingside, there is a danger of seeing his queenside majority struggle, too, so Black does more tidying. The original matter of the damaged kingside is no longer the problem now that White's army has been held at bay and slimmed down a little, but it is important for Black to remain circumspect.

33 Re3

33 Bxg7+ Kxg7 34 Rxe8 Rxe8 35 cxb4 Re4 36 Ra4 is hardly what White would consider a promising ending.

33...bxc3 34 bxc3 Rxe3+ 35 Kxe3 Re8+ 36 Kd3 Bxd4 37 cxd4 Kg7 38 Ra7 Re1 (Diagram 28)

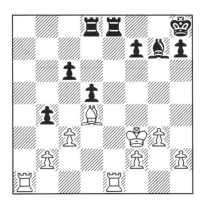

Diagram 27
Position after 32...b4

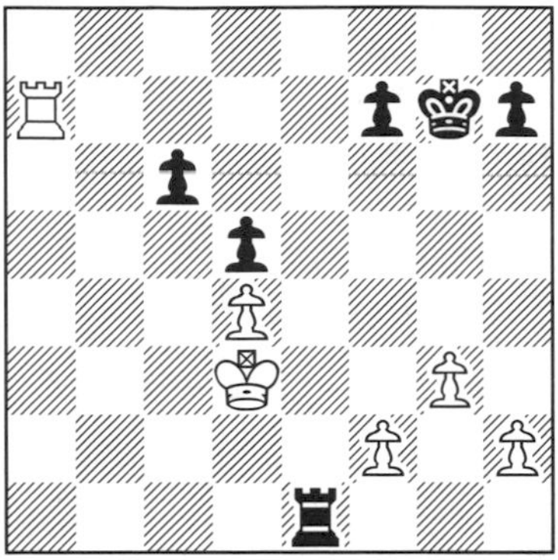

Diagram 28
Position after 38...Re1

White has the more active king but the game is drawn because Black's king, for example, happens to be doing a good job where it stands, while Black's rook is busy.

39 Rc7 Rd1+ 40 Ke3 Re1+ 41 Kd2 Rf1 42 Ke2 Rc1 43 h4 h5 44 Kf3 Kg6 ½-½

Another good example of competent chess.

Finally, here's a nice demonstration of not being at all intimidated by your opponent's kingside onslaught.

□ **S.Sarno** ■ **O.Touzane**

Mitropa Cup, Leipzig 2002

1 c4 Nf6 2 Nc3 g6 3 g3 Bg7 4 Bg2 0-0 5 Nf3 d6 6 0-0 Nc6 7 d3 e5 (Diagram 29)

Both players have set out their stalls. White's forces are primed for a queenside offensive, while Black is given an opportunity to get going on the kingside.

8 Rb1 a5 9 a3 h6

Black's strategy revolves around making his presence felt in front of White's king with ...Bh3, so the text simply rules out Ng5 in reply to the preparatory ...Be6. Nudging the h-pawn also prevents Bg5xNf6 (an exchange that can help White), as well as facilitating a future attacking push with ...g6-g5.

10 b4 axb4 11 axb4 Be6 12 b5 Ne7 13 Bb2 Qd7 14 Re1 (Diagram 30)

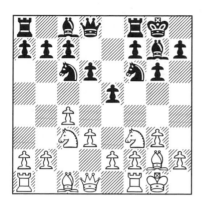

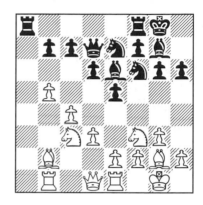

Diagram 29
Position after 7...e5

Diagram 30
Position after 14 Re1

Each player has his own agenda, and thus far the game has a very respectable, textbook air. But now, with development being completed, we are entering a new phase in which important decisions must be made. The first revolves around White's fianchetto. The bishop both helps protect the king and exerts pressure on the enemy queenside, so it would make sense to avoid parting with it – hence the text, which prevents the pin on the short diagonal.

14...Bh3 15 Bh1

As we shall see, White appears to pay quite a price for the survival of his favourite bishop.

15...Ng4

Having established the bishop on h3, Black sends another piece toward the enemy king, freeing the f-pawn in the process. I guess that most club players would already prefer to be sitting on Black's side of the board here. The player defending his king in mutual (flank) attacking situations does have more to lose in terms of the more serious implications of a mistake, but this doesn't mean we should be afraid of seeing our king come under pressure. In fact a willingness to do so brings rewards as long there is sufficient confidence not to be intimidated while applying pressure on the opposition elsewhere. Watch how Sarno holds strong in this game.

16 Qb3 Kh8

Tucking the king away from the a2-g8 diagonal in preparation of the launch of the f7-pawn. This might seem like a standard sidestep but it matters where the king goes, as Touzane had found out to his cost a year earlier in V.Anand-O.Touzane, Moscow 2001: 16...Kh7 17 Ne4! and White suddenly had two knights ready to deliver a nasty fork on g5. Black's best might well be to face facts and drop the king back to h8, but instead Touzane tried to justify his play, and the game continued 17...Qf5? 18 b6! Qh5 19 bxc7 f5 20 Nxd6 f4 21 Qxb7 fxg3 22 hxg3 Bf1 with a similar theme to the main game, Anand simply mopping up with 23 Nh4 g5 24 Qe4+ Kg8 25 Bf3 Bh3 26 Bxg4 Bxg4 27 Ng2 Ra6 28 Bxe5 1-0.

17 Ra1 (Diagram 31)

Diagram 31	Diagram 32
Position after 17 Ra1	Position after 20 Rec1

Contesting the a-file and tempting Black into trading off an important defender.

17...Rab8

The immediate 17...f5!? is possible but Black prefers to address the queenside first.

90

18 Nd5

Either White is allowed an advanced, central knight or a new avenue on the c-file.

18...Nxd5?!

The '?!' is from Ribli, whose proposed 18...f5!? does look better, if only to temporarily deny White use of the c-file.

19 cxd5 f5 20 Rec1 (Diagram 32)

White does have the queenside in his sights but his kingside is coming under pressure from pieces and pawns. In fact this is another position that would attract more club players to Black's side of the board thanks to his more menacing looking build-up of forces. Furthermore, it appears that when the temperature hots up on the kingside White will be short of defenders.

20...f4

Obvious and easy play from Black.

21 Ra4!

But White's latest is far from obvious.

21...g5 22 Rac4 fxg3 23 hxg3

Not 23 Rxc7 gxf2 mate.

23...Qf7?

This might seem like a careless mistake – that's because it is – yet it is also typical of players who put too much stock in kingside attacks to give the opposition's counterplay insufficient respect. In this case Black doesn't bother with 23...Rbc8 24 b6, which is a much lesser evil but one that would switch the action to an area of the board where White has the undisputed upper hand. Instead Black heads over to his target.

24 Rxc7 Qh5 25 Qb4! Bf1 (Diagram 33)

The point, and a motif we saw in Touzane's game against Anand. The bishop is immune to capture as 26 Kxf1?? walks into immediate mate and 26 Rxf1 Rxf3 leaves the king trapped and ...Qh2+ (mate) coming. It is always nice to play such moves, and perhaps Black's confidence was boosted by his anticipation of putting his opponent under additional pressure, which might further explain why he was willing to give ground on the other flank.

26 Qe1!

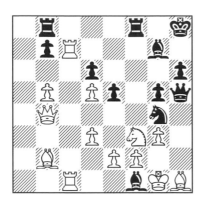

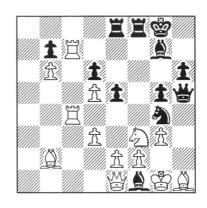

Diagram 33
Position after 25...Bf1

Diagram 34
Position after 28 R1c4!

The calm switch with Q(b3)-b4-e1 is an unlikely defensive resource but one which I hope will serve to give the reader confidence when it comes to defending against an attack on the king. Many club players' simplistic view of attacking and defending prevents them from taking up openings and variations such as this line of the English because the prospect of coming under fierce attack while pinpointing a weakness in the enemy queenside seems too risky. But there tend to be more defensive possibilities than meet the eye, and it is a matter of looking out for ways in which the king can be supported and the opposition's often blunt attempts at breaking through prevented or rendered harmless. The modern 'get results' quickly attitude throws all sorts of entertaining, attacking wins our way, page after page, without so much as giving the victim a chance of survival, but it defies logic to think that the defender doesn't enjoy the same level of flexibility, that easy-to-create threats can't generally be dealt with through calm, common sense measures.

The arrival of the queen adds crucial protection to f2. Now 26...Rxf3 27 Bxf3? Qh2+ 28 Kxf1 seems to hold for White but 28...Rf8! reapplies the pressure and is in fact enough to force a draw, e.g. 29 Rc8 (29 e3 Rxf3 and 29 e4 Rxf3 put White in trouble) 29...Ne3+ 30 fxe3 Qh1+ 31 Kf2 Qh2+ 32 Kf1, or 29...Qh3+ 30 Kg1 Qh2+ 31 Kf1 Qh3+ as 32 Bg2?? Ne3+ is the end. However, after 27 exf3 Qh2+ 28 Kxf1 Qxh1+ 29 Ke2 Black is losing. Note in this line that Black's advanced, menacing pieces enjoy a flurry of activity from which White emerges with a decisive advantage.

26...Kg8

I suspect that – with valuable time ticking away (Touzane is one of the quickest players I've ever seen) – this was intended to make the point that the cheeky bishop is still safe on f1.

27 b6

A nice move which is indicative of White's confidence that his kingside is ready to withstand any further blows from Black.

27...Rbe8 28 R1c4! (Diagram 34)

With every one of Black's outfield pieces now on the kingside, primed for an all-out assault, White continues work on the other flank. But the text is another excellent defensive move, monitoring the important knight on g4. Like the transfer of the queen to e1, defending along the fourth rank is another facet of White's technique that most club players would at best describe as unconventional.

TIP: When holding an advantage in one area of the board while defending the king in the face of intimidating play, the trick is to see through the haze of the opposition's phantom threats and possibilities and home in how the genuine threats can be neutralised.

28...Bh3

By introducing Rxg4 as an option White sends the bishop packing.

29 Rxb7

The demolition of Black's queenside continues. Does White have everything under control?

29..Bh8

Setting up ...e5-e4, which is currently impossible due to Rxg7+ etc.

30 Rcc7!? Bf1 (Diagram 35)

Note how Black has played almost exclusively on the kingside, during which time White has hardly touched his pieces in this sector, other than shifting his rook from f1, dropping the bishop back to the passive looking h1 outpost and placing the queen on e1. If it's not broken, don't fix it. In the meantime, White owns the queenside. On seeing the rook vacate the fourth rank Black plants his bishop back on f1, once again clearing the path for the queen. With 30...e4 still unavailable in view of 31 Rg7+, there is little else Black can do.

31 Re7

By now we should all be well aware that 31 Qxf1? walks into 31...Rxf3.

31...Rxe7 32 Rxe7 e4 33 Rxe4

Black has looked dangerous throughout, yet White has defended in such a way that the bark has always been much worse than the bite. Equally effective is 33 Bxh8, e.g. 33...exf3 34 Bxf3 Rxf3 35 exf3 or 33...Rxf3 34 Bxf3 exf3 35 exf3.

33...Bxb2

33...Rxf3 gets Black nowhere after either recapture.

34 Qxf1 Rxf3 35 Rxg4 (Diagram 36)

Diagram 35
Position after 30...Bf1

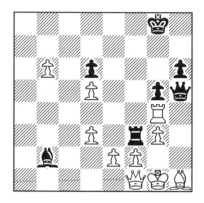

Diagram 36
Position after 35 Rxg4

Despite venturing all over the place the rook finally comes to the rescue with this crucial (albeit, by now, rather obvious) elimination of the knight.

35...Rxd3

35...Qxg4 36 Bxf3 Qb4 37 Qh3 Qxb6 38 Qc8+! Kg7 39 Qd7+ Kg8 40 Bh5 Qb8 41 Qe6+ and the h6-pawn will drop with check.

36 Rb4 Bc3 37 b7 1-0

White's bishop still sits on h1, and his queen has spent most of the game further overseeing events in the kingside. Thanks to White's faith in the strength of his defences he was able to push through his lead on the queenside. Black could have put up more resistance there but, like so many others, overestimated his kingside attack. It is worth noting that Touzane is an aggressive IM with numerous big scalps to his name, yet his vigorous attempts to break through came to nothing despite his opponent hardly reacting to the pressure.

Chapter Four

Relocation

One of the most flexible yet under-used defensive tools is the relocation of a piece. This might be, for example, a transfer of a piece from a redundant post to a better one, escaping the danger area or giving a hitherto attacking piece urgent defensive duties. However, whether or not changing the direction of your play or relocating a piece works is often not the key issue in a difficult situation. Rather it is the realisation that something drastic needs to be done to avoid otherwise imminent defeat. Remember that soldiering on without a fight when the opposition's attacking task is too easy for him to err is tantamount to resignation.

> **NOTE: Don't be afraid to approach a problem from another angle by designating a particular piece with a last-ditch role.**

Switching Files

In our first example Black induces a committal pawn advance on one file and then switches to the neighbouring file with great effect.

☐ **E.Cekro** ■ **Z.Bogut**

Bosnia-Herzogovina Team Championship 2002

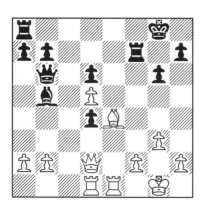

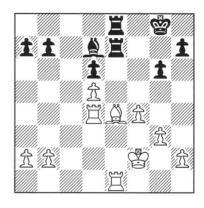

Diagram 1
Position after 25 Rcd1

Diagram 2
Position after 29...Bd7

If d4 drops Black will have nothing to show for the pawn deficit. Time for a instructive example of switching.

25...Raf8!?

A good old-fashioned threat to unsettle White.

26 f4?!

26 f3 avoids all that follows, although after 26...d3+ Black seems to be okay, e.g. 27 Kg2 (assessed by Ribli as slightly better for White) 27...Rc8, or 27 Qe3 Qxe3+ 28 Rxe3 Re8 29 Kf2 Rfe7 30 Rc1. At least with the bishop bolted on to e4 White is solid and can perhaps look forward to eventually picking off the d3-pawn, whereas after the text the e-file is too much of a distraction.

26...Re7

26...d3+ 27 Qe3? Qxe3+ 28 Rxe3 Re8 29 Kf2 Rfe7 30 Kf3 Bc4 31 b3 Rxe4 works out well for Black, but the sensible 27 Kg2 Qd4 28 Qf2 is about even. The text is the beginning of a powerful relocation of Black's rooks that (thanks to White's rather careless f2-f4) soon has White tied up.

27 Qxd4 Qxd4+ 28 Rxd4 Rfe8 29 Kf2 Bd7 (Diagram 2)

White has pocketed the pawn but at some cost, with the pin becoming increasingly troublesome. In fact the pressure is about to increase because another relocation from Black will see the bishop transfer to f5.

30 Kf3 h5!

Black makes sure to rule out g3-g4 before cementing his bishop on the optimum f5-posting. Consequently the problem with the pin will prove more significant than the extra pawn, and there is, in fact, nothing White can do about it.

31 Ke3 Bf5 32 Kd3 Kg7 33 a4 b6

Black has set his stall out and can simply maintain the bind with 'passing' moves. 33...a5, for example, would be equally effective.

34 Rc4 Kf6 35 h4 Kg7 36 Re3

36 b4 Kf6 37 b5 Kg7 gets White nowhere.

36...a5 37 Re1 Kf6 ½-½

Black's alert doubling on the f-file was enough to negate the potential weakness of the front d-pawn. Note how White's f2-f4 looked more solid than the superior f2-f3.

Make or Break

Biting the bullet and being prepared to allow the opposition's attack to gain momentum by your sending a key defender elsewhere to help in launching a counter-offensive is a difficult concept to get to grips with, but it is one that can save – and generate – points.

□ S.Klimov ■ V.Loginov
St. Petersburg Championship 2002

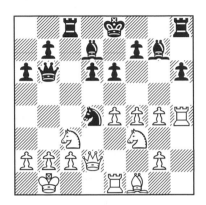

Diagram 3	Diagram 4
Position after 16...Nd4	Position after 19 f5

White is a pawn up in this by no means untypical Sicilian, opposite sides castling scenario, but Black is looking to the dark squares – in particular the long-range bishop – for compensation. 17 Nxd4 Qxd4 18 Qxd4 Bxd4 19 Nd1 Ke7 leaves White with just an edge thanks to the modest material lead. Klimov opts for an uncompromising try for more.

17 e5!

By closing out the long diagonal White does his king a favour, while any hand-to-hand combat in the centre or on the kingside is sure to unsettle Black's king.

17...Nxf3 18 gxf3 d5

18...Bc6 19 Ne4 (19 Qxd6? Qf2) 19...Bxe4 20 Rxe4 is an easy, clear advantage for White.

19 f5 (Diagram 4)

White puts the extra pawn to good use and further tightens the screw on the kingside. In fact Black's stock has quickly dropped, and he now has nothing to show for the pawn. One way to hit back could be with 19...d4, but after the promising looking 20 Ne4 Bxe5 21 Rxh6 Rxh6 22 Qxh6 d3 (Black's best here is 22...Qb4! 23 Rd1, although White is in

control, e.g. 23...exf5 24 Nf6+) 23 c3 Rxc3 White has 24 Nf6+! as
24...Bxf6 25 Qxf6 d2 26 Qh8+! Ke7 27 f6+ Kd6 28 Qh2+ mops up the
pawn, 24...Kd8 25 Qh8+ Kc7 walks into 26 Nd5+! and 24...Ke7 25
Nd5+! **(Diagram 5)** is even funnier.

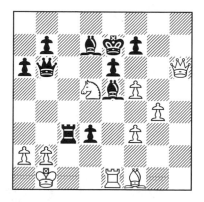

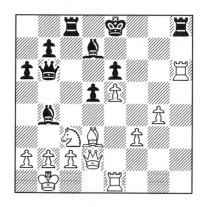

Diagram 5	**Diagram 6**
Position after 25 Nd5+!	Position after 22 Rxh6

19...Bf8!

I like this move – not because it denies White his claim to an advantage
(it doesn't) but because Black is saying that if White is insisting on attacking on the kingside he will have to take his medicine on the queenside. As we shall see White could avoid any potential banana skins con-
cerning his king but his aggressive play thus far suggests that he is no
mood to decelerate.

20 fxe6 fxe6 21 Bd3?!

In view of how the game has developed since we joined it, anything else
just wouldn't look fitting. White used the front f-pawn to chip away at
Black's already damaged defensive wall and now there is a gaping hole
on g6 that was tailor made for the bishop. White allows the coming pin
because the bishop's absence from the kingside permits a subsequent
invasion, which is why – understandably – White was averse to
wimping out with 21 Nd1, which takes the sting out of ...Bb4 and alters
the texture of the game to one in which the extra pawn is the most important feature. Note that the text is absolutely fine with best play, but
remember how often practical considerations demote best play to a minor role.

21...Bb4 22 Rxh6 (Diagram 6) 22...Rg8

Of course Black has had to abandon the kingside in his endeavour to switch the play and generate threats of his own, but parting with the remaining 'defender' would be going too far: 22...Rxh6? 23 Qxh6 Bxc3 24 Qh8+ Kf7 25 Bg6+! Kxg6 26 Qf6+ Kh7 27 Rh1+ with mate next move.

23 Kc1

Sidestepping any serious pin on the b-file.

23...d4

Exploiting another pin.

24 Qf2

And there's another pin...

24...Qa5 (Diagram 7)

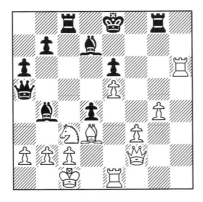

Diagram 7
Position after 24...Qa5

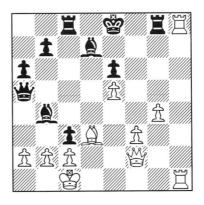

Diagram 8
Position after 26 Rh8

At the risk of over-using the word 'pin', Black's relocation of the once well-placed then closed out bishop has helped him whip up some awkward counterplay in the shape of the pinned knight. The diagram position throws up an important psychological scenario regarding how both players tend to 'see' the same possibilities and the subsequent evaluations that follow at the critical points of a tense game such as this. It is safe to assume at this level that both players were not playing move by move, rather that a certain amount of planning was involved. Consequently, when this position will have been analysed it would have been easy for White to stop at 25 Qxd4(!) 25...Rxc3 (26 bxc3 Bxc3) in favour of White's choice in the game, but there is the unlikely cheeky move found by Tyomkin: 26 Rd1!, when the (currently obstructed!) d-file is a big problem for Black, e.g. 26...Rc7 (26...Rxd3 27 Qxd3 Bc8 [27...Qc7 28 Qh7! Rf8 29 Rxe6+ Kd8 30 Red6 Bxd6 31 exd6 and 32 Qe7+] 28 Qh7 Rf8 29 Qg6+ Rf7 30 Rh7 Qc7 31 Rd6!) 27 Bc4 Be7 28 Bxe6 etc. Whether Black saw 26 Rd1! is irrelevant. What matters is that his uncompromising play involving ...B(g7)-f8-b4 is about to help steer White in a particular direction that Black is happy to follow.

 TIP: Increasing the number of complicated possibilities available to both sides – even if best play ultimately loses – is preferable to the futile policy of passive 'defence' against the opposition's effortless, risk-free initiative.

25 Reh1?

Sending the heavy artillery to attack Black's ravaged kingside has obviously been part of White's plan all along, but the text is, in fact, good enough only for a draw.

25...dxc3 26 Rh8 (Diagram 8) 26...Qxa2!

End-to-end action, as the soccer pundits would say. 26...Rxh8? loses to 27 Rxh8+, e.g. 27...Bf8 (27...Kf7 28 Rh7+ Kg8 29 Qe3 or 29 Qh2 leads to forced mate) 28 Bg6+ Kd8 29 Rxf8+ Kc7 30 Qd4 cxb2+ 31 Kxb2 Qb5+ 32 Kc1 Rxf8 33 Qd6+ Kc8 34 Qxf8+ Kc7 35 Qd6+ Kc8 36 Be4. The text, on the other hand, gives White no time to exploit his enormous firepower due to the threat of mate.

27 Rxg8+ Kf7

27...Bf8 28 Bg6+ Kd8 29 Qb6+ with mate to follow.

28 Rg7+! (Diagram 9)

Now it is White's turn to dig for defensive resources.

28...Kxg7

28...Kf8 29 Rh8+ is a fun way of forcing Black to accept the 'gift' and transpose to the game.

29 Rh7+

Tyomkin writes that it is a pity White has no more than a draw, but I think Black deserves credit for generating sufficient counter-chances to induce such entertaining play. After the initial 17 e5 White had an extra pawn and the makings of a dangerous looking breakthrough on the kingside – we could expect only one-way traffic. Yet Black homed in on the essence of the struggle (White's promising initiative), skilfully helping White's attack along by introducing counterplay on the queenside.

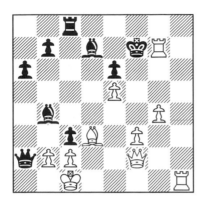

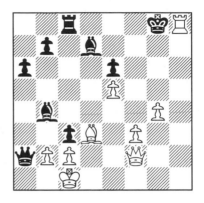

Diagram 9	**Diagram 10**
Position after 28 Rg7+!	Position after 32 Rh8+

29...Kg8 30 Rh8+!

That White can sacrifice both rooks and still draw is indicative of just how much he owned the kingside. Black declines, but the result won't change.

30...Kg7

Black declines the sacrifice but now it's perpetual. 30...Kxh8 31 Qh4+ Kg8 32 Qg5+ Kf8 33 Qf6+ Kg8 is an alternative finish.

31 Rh7+ Kg8 32 Rh8+ (Diagram 10) 32...Kg7 ½-½

The Flexible Knight

A poor knight can soon become an excellent one thanks to the facility to hop around from one colour complex to another. Watch how Black neutralises his opponent's space advantage with a good bit of regrouping.

□ **L.Bruzon** ■ **Y.Gonzalez**

Cuban Championship 2002

For the moment Black's king is safest in the centre as each white rook enjoys a ready-made open file. Meanwhile, Black is also fairly cramped and needs to develop.

17...Ng6 18 Bd2 Be7 19 Qe2

Sensible play from White, who is toying with the idea of castling queenside in anticipation of Black's king going the other way. 19 Ne3 f6! 20 Nf5 0-0, on the other hand, favours Black.

19...Nf8! (Diagram 12)

Diagram 11	**Diagram 12**
Position after 17 Nxg2	Position after 19...Nf8!

19...0-0 20 g5 looks too risky for Black in view of White's easy use of the h-file. The text has the dual advantage of improving a key piece and keeping White guessing as to where the king will go.

20 Nh4

Black's previous moves allows him to meet 20 Ne3 with 20...g6 to prevent Nf5.

20...Bxh4

While this trade is not strictly necessary it does alleviate some of the pressure by reducing White's potentially dangerous attacking force. Black also judges that his knight will be just as good as White's remaining bishop, which is hampered by its own pawns. Hopefully this should compensate for White's territorial supremacy and menacing major pieces.

21 Rxh4

21 gxh4 looks preferable to me considering how things might pan out in the long-term, but White likes his open lines.

21...h6 22 0-0-0

22 g5 Ng6 23 Rh5 hxg5 24 Rxh8+ Nxh8 sees the knight continue its journey, although after 25 Bxg5 Qf5 26 Be3 Ng6 it returns to the fold

and Black's influence on the light squares secures a balanced game.

22...0-0-0

The knight manoeuvre has effectively allowed Black to play a waiting game, resulting in his being able to hold back the king until White runs out of constructive alternatives to committing his own.

23 Rh5 Ne6 (Diagram 13)

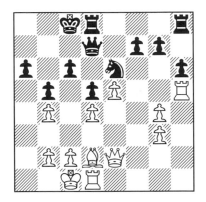

Diagram 13	Diagram 14
Position after 23...Ne6	Position after 28 b3

Black's queenside structure isn't great but nor is White's, and Black's endeavours to find the optimum post for his knight has been successful enough to render White's attacking stance rather toothless. White makes a token show of aggression on the kingside, but Black is ready.

24 Qf2 Qa7 25 Be3

Note that Black is giving White a reason to play c2-c3, which would do the bishop no favours and even add weight to a future ...a6-a5 break by weakening the light squares in front of White's king.

25...Rhf8 26 Rf5 Rd7

Over-protection.

27 Qd2 Qc7 28 b3 ½-½ (Diagram 14)

White is obviously the more active of the two here, but he is unable to make any progress – thanks in no small part to the fantastic knight. Had Black not carried out this transfer to e6 it would have been a different story.

Endgame Transformation

Not surprisingly, the fewer pieces that remain in play, the more important it is to get the most from what we have left, which is why a transfer of a piece in the ending can be particularly worthwhile from a defensive point of view. In the ending below Black's bishop works overtime to save the day.

□ **L.Milov** ■ **S.Galdunts**

Griesheim 2002

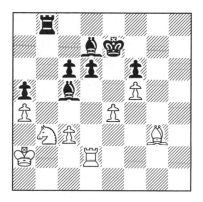

Diagram 15
Position after 46 Rxd2

Diagram 16
Position after 50 Re2

I used this game in another of my books a while ago but made a note of Black's excellent defence in case I found myself writing a book on the subject. The first thing we notice in the diagram position is White's pressure on the h2-b8 diagonal, where White in fact threatens Nxc5 due to the pin against the rook. This helps Black find the first part of an impressive defence.

46...Rg8! 47 Bh2 Rg4

Black would like to keep his dark-squared bishop on the board but d6 needs protecting, so instead he further activates his rook.

48 Nxc5 dxc5 49 Bd6+ Ke8 50 Re2 (Diagram 16)

Material is level but the presence of the pair of rooks means that White can make life very difficult for his opponent, the inability to challenge the dominant bishop being a key feature of rook and opposite coloured

105

bishop endings. Many club players fail to properly appreciate this and mistakenly expect the ending to peter out to a draw (which is often the case when only the bishops are involved), but Black must seek to improve his lot or be forced into uncomfortable passivity.

50...Bc8!

Black knows that finding a more aggressive role for his bishop takes priority over the futile ...c5-c4 (which may well make matters worse).

51 Kb3 Ba6 52 Re3 Bf1

This transfer goes a long way to achieving equality, which is White tries to avoid by maintaining the tension.

53 c4!? (Diagram 17)

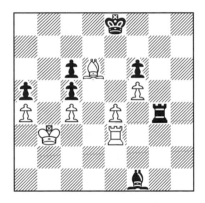 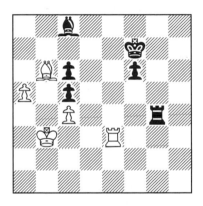

Diagram 17
Position after 53 c4!?

Diagram 18
Position after 57...Bc8

An interesting try that is better than the automatic 53 Bxc5?! Bg2 54 e5 Bd5+ when the excellent bishop outweighs the pawn deficit. Incidentally, White could walk straight into trouble in the event of 55 Ka3? Rg2 56 exf6+ Kf7, when the mate threat on a2 would force 57 c4 Bxc4 58 Rb3 etc. Note how this appeared to come from nowhere – defending doesn't mean that you should forget to keep your eyes peeled for winning possibilities.

53...Kf7!

Admit it – you would have played 53...Bg2 automatically. You might even have gone as far as working out that the subsequent 54 e5 fxe5 55 Rxe5+ Kd7 56 Bxc5? Re4 forces off the rooks. However, after the less obvious 56 Bf8 White's rook is free to whip off the c5-pawn, after which a5 is ripe for the taking. The text avoids a check in the event of e4-e5 and subsequent captures.

54 Bc7 Bg2 55 e5

Just as one mistake tends to lead to another, good play has a nice habit of rewarding us with what seem like fortuitous circumstances. In this case there is the line 55 Bxa5 Bxe4 56 Bb6 Bxf5 57 a5 Bc8 **(Diagram 18)**.

Coming full circle, the bishop returns to the queenside in time to halt White's new passed pawn, securing equality in the process. Whether Black managed to find this when he sent the bishop on its initial quest we'll never know, but it seems fitting that the bishop would have been able to come to the rescue after helping resolve the situation in the centre.

55...fxe5 56 Bxe5 Re4! (Diagram 19)

Diagram 19
Position after 56...Re4!

Diagram 20
Position after 63...Bd1+

TIP: The defender in rook and opposite coloured bishop endings should strive to engineer a situation in which the last pair of rooks is exchanged, even at the cost of a pawn (or more) if necessary.

With only one bishop to watch over the task is so much easier, as the defender should then have a whole colour complex under control (the attacker's rook might not only contest the influence of the defending bishop but also combine with the bishop to generate threats that would otherwise not exist).

57 Rxe4 Bxe4 58 f6

White has a protected passed pawn but needs to create a second front if Black is to be tested.

58...Bf3! 59 Bc3 Bd1+ 60 Ka3 Be2 61 Bxa5 Kxf6 62 Bd8+ Ke6 63 Kb3 Bd1+ ½-½ (Diagram 20)

Black's bishop has the last word. Notice in this example that White was the one trying to generate winning chances but Black had his fair share of the play thanks to his hitherto dormant bishop.

Chapter Five

Holding On

Some players dread coming under attack or being on the back foot in a difficult position, having such a defeatist attitude that they see the game (and any share of it) drifting away as soon as the defensive barrier is broken, for example. We want to be part of a more stubborn group of players who hang on in there and strive to put up maximum resistance.

Hanging on by your Fingernails...

Sometimes it is necessary to stand toe-to-toe with your opponent even when things are not going your way – or, as we can see elsewhere in these pages, especially when things are not going your way.

☐ **G.Kacheishvili** ■ **A.Shabalov**

Denver 2002

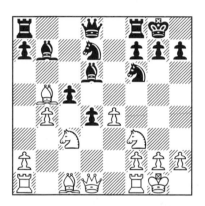

Diagram 1
Position after 12...0-0!

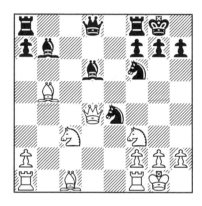

Diagram 2
Position after 14...Ncxe4

The diagram position arose after the following opening moves:

1 d4 Nf6 2 c4 e6 3 Nf3 b6 4 e3 Bb7 5 Bd3 d5 6 0-0 c5 7 cxd5 exd5 8 Nc3 Bd6!? 9 dxc5 bxc5 10 Bb5+ Nbd7 11 e4 d4 12 b4 0-0! (Diagram 1)

White has lost his way somewhere along the line (perhaps an early b2-b3 was called for, rather than committing himself in the centre) and already has problems because the coming clearance of the centre pawns will leave Black with the more menacing set-up.

13 bxc5 Nxc5 14 Qxd4 Ncxe4 (Diagram 2)

White's forces are far from ideally placed and he lags behind in development; even his king is in the firing line of Black's bishops. Without analysing anything specific, we get the impression that White is skating on thin ice, lacking a proper foothold on the position. A strong player's initial feeling here would be one of apprehension, that White might already be unable to deal even with fairly standard, not too subtle threats. For example 15 Bb2 looks sensible enough but 15...Ng5! exerts immediate pressure (16 Nxg5? Bxh2+ and 17...Qxd4): 16 Ne5 a6 17 Ba4 Qb8! 18 Nd1 (18 f4 Bxg2) 18...Ne6 19 Qe3 Nd5 20 Qe1 Nc5 (Black continues to make progress at White's expense) 21 Bc2 Re8 etc. Notice how White was pushed back by Black's more harmonious forces.

15 Nxe4

The best practical chance, trading an average knight for a more dangerous one, in the process preparing to reinforce the a1-h8 diagonal.

15...Bxe4 16 Bb2 (Diagram 3)

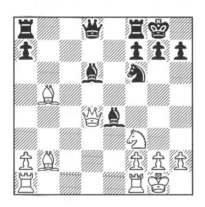

Diagram 3
Position after 16 Bb2

Diagram 4
Position after 19...Rb4

Another good choice. The alternative is 16 Ne5 but again White is teetering on the edge, as can be seen from the following lines: 16...Rb8 17 a4 a6 18 Bc4 (18 Bxa6 Rb4) 18...Qc7 19 Ng4 (19 Bf4 Rbe8 20 Nxf7 Bxf4 21 Nd6+ Kh8 22 Nxe8 Bxh2+ 23 Kh1 Rxe8) 19...Nxg4 20 Qxe4 Rb4 21 Qxg4 Bxh2+ 22 Kh1 Be5 (22...Rxc4? 23 f4) 23 Bb2 Bxb2 24 Bxf7+ Rxf7 25 Qxb4 Bxa1 26 Rxa1 Rxf2 etc.

The advantage of 16 Bb2 is that it improves White's game (completing development) and – in a position that is anyway considerably worse – gives Black a choice between taking a clear advantage (correct) or trying for more (incorrect).

> **TIP:** If it is evident that you should be clearly worse with best play, don't enter into a forcing line when a useful but non-committal option is available, thus putting the onus on the opponent to make the right decision (rather than doing it for him).

16...Rb8

The simplest route to a healthy advantage is 16...Qb8 17 Qa4 Bxf3 18 Bxf6 Bh5 19 Bg5 Bxh2+ 20 Kh1 Be5 (as I always say – a pawn is a pawn), but Black has more ambitious plans. This is good news for White because – unless he enjoys being a pawn down with a weakened king position and absolutely no counterplay – anything that mixes it up a little is a preferable scenario. The decision he is soon going to regret.

17 a4 a6 18 Nd2 Bd5 19 Bc4 Rb4 (Diagram 4)

This is what Black had in mind, and he is about to take a points lead. However, it transpires that the circumstances of his material gain afford White some important spoiling tactics.

20 Rfd1! Qc7 21 Bc3 Rxc4 22 Nxc4 Bxh2+

22...Bc5? 23 Qh4 Bxc4 and now instead of the losing 24 Qxc4?? Bxf2+ White has 24 Rac1, e.g. 24...Ne8 25 Bxg7 Nxg7 26 Qxc4 Ne627 Qxa6, or 26...Rc8 27 Qxc5 Qxc5 28 Rxc5 Rxc5 29 Rd8+ Ne8 30 Rxe8+ Kg7 31 f3 etc.

23 Kh1 Bxc4 24 Qh4! (Diagram 5)

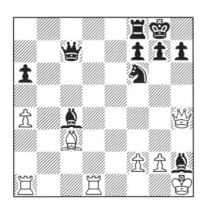

Diagram 5
Position after 24 Qh4!

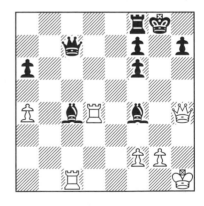

Diagram 6
Position after 27 Rd4!

White plays his Get Out of Jail Free card. Suddenly Black's pieces find themselves walking a tightrope thanks to the coming exchange on f6, which in turn leaves Black's king exposed.

24...Bd6

24...Nd5 25 Qxh2 Qxh2+ 26 Kxh2 Nxc3 27 Rdc1 Ne4 28 Rxc4 Nxf2 29 Re1 favours the rooks.

25 Bxf6 gxf6 26 Rac1 Bf4 27 Rd4! (Diagram 6)

Now White gets to push Black around a little before forcing the draw, as Black is unable to keep hold of both bishops.

27...Bxc1 ½-½

The draw results from 28 Rg4+ Bg5 29 Rxg5+ fxg5 (29...Kh8?? 30 Qh6) 30 Qxg5+ Kh8 31 Qf6+ Kg8 32 Qg5+ etc. White was behind from the beginning but managed to catch up at the end, thanks first to his persistence and then to his deliberately retaining the very tension that defined Black's advantage, in order not to provide his opponent with an easy route to conversion. There was sufficient energy in White's position to pounce.

Some attacks start and finish very quickly. This could be because everything goes right (for the aggressor) or wrong (completely unsound), but often the defender will fail to withstand the pressure. If the opposition's attack is strong and sound and he follows through well, then so be it, but there's little point in sitting down to play if we donate points and half-points by failing to test the attacker's judgement. One of the characteristics that differentiates top players from club players is this quality to doggedly keep up with the pace. Apart from the obvious potentially beneficial implications it is worth noting that, from a psychological point of view, earning just a slight advantage after trying so hard for a knockout blow is not enough for most players. Many opponents will be neither willing nor able to start a new, long struggle, and continued resistance on your part should make the draw more likely than would be the case if the attack never took place.

□ **J.Timman** ■ **J.Lautier**

Ubeda 1997

White is a pawn down but has a development lead and his forces are menacingly posted. Black's king is still in the middle. We know what's coming.

20 Nxe6! fxe6 21 Bxe6 Kf8!

Already Black needs to be careful. 21...Ne4 22 Bb3 backfires, while 21...Qe7 22 Rfe1 Kf8 23 Qb6! Bxf3 24 Rc7 Qb4 25 Rf7+ Ke8 26 Re5! wins for White. Better to get the king off the e-file.

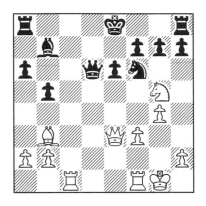

Diagram 7
Position after 19...Qd6

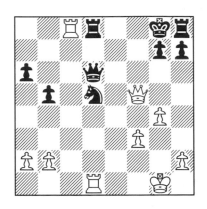

Diagram 8
Position after 26 Rc8!

22 Rfd1 Qe7

22...Nd5 23 Bxd5 Bxd5 24 Rc5 is awful for Black, while 22...Bd5 runs into trouble after 23 Bxd5 Nxd5 24 Qe4 (White can do much better than 24 Qd4?! Re8! 25 Qxd5 Re1+ 26 Kf2 Qxd5 27 Rc8+ Ke7 28 Rc7+ Kd6 29 Rxd5+ Kxc7 30 Kxe1) 24...Rd8 25 Qf5+, e.g. 25...Qf6 26 Rxd5, 25...Ke8 26 Rxd5! Qxd5 27 Re1+, or 25...Kg8 26 Rc8! **(Diagram 8)**. This is a typical example of Black not coping properly. The extra rook sits locked away on h8 so in the real battle Black is an exchange down, and the back rank is creaking. After the subsequent 26...Rxc8 27 Qxc8+ Kf7 28 Qf5+ (28 Qxh8? Qc5+) 28...Qf6 29 Qxd5+ Qe6 30 Qd7+ Qxd7 31 Rxd7+ Kf6 32 Rd6+ the ending is hopeless for Black. The text avoids all this and has the added advantage of pinning the bishop.

23 g5

Keeping the pressure on. 23 Qb6? Bxf3 24 Rc7 Bxd1 25 Rxe7 Kxe7 leaves White outnumbered.

23...Re8

This time 23...Nd5? 24 Rxd5 Bxd5 25 Qf4+ Ke8 26 Bxd5 Rd8 27 Bc6+ Rd7 28 Bxd7+ Qxd7 29 Qe5+ is final, as is 23...Bd5 24 gxf6 Qxe6 25 fxg7+ Kxg7 26 Rc7+ etc.

24 gxf6 (Diagram 9)

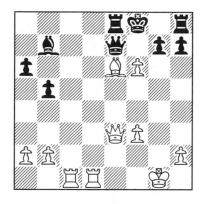

Diagram 9
Position after 24 gxf6

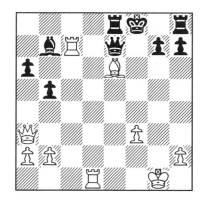

Diagram 10
Position after 26 Rc7!

Winning back the piece and putting Black at yet another awkward crossroads. Which of the three choices (...Qxe6, ...Qxf6 and ...gxf6) is best?

24...gxf6

Correct. After 24...Qxf6 there comes 25 Qa3+! Qe7 26 Rc7! **(Diagram 10)**.

Then 26...Qxa3 (26...b4 27 Qxb4!!) 27 Rf7+ Kg8 28 Rf6+ Rxe6 29 Rd8+ is a nice mate. Meanwhile, 24...Qxe6 25 Qxe6 Rxe6 26 Rd7 gxf6 27 Rxb7 Rg8+ 28 Kf2 brings about a double rook ending where material is level but with a near decisive advantage to White (try it out for yourself). After the text Black is still struggling a little but at least he has tidied up, and now the g-file is ready for a welcome check. Perhaps this was going through White's mind in selecting his next.

25 Qh6+

This is tempting in that White can convert one promising advantage for another, but White could have let the dormant rook into the game and still been firmly in the driving seat: 25 Re1! Rg8+ 26 Kf2 Rg7 (26...Rg5? 27 Qf4 Qg7 28 Bg4! Rge5 29 Rxe5 Rxe5 30 Rd1 Qe7 31 Rd7 Re2+ 32 Kg3) 27 Qf4 Qd8 28 Rc5 and Black is still under pressure despite all his pieces now being 'involved' in the game.

25...Qg7+ 26 Qxg7+ Kxg7 27 Rc7+ Kh6 (Diagram 11)

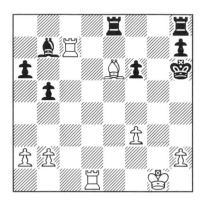

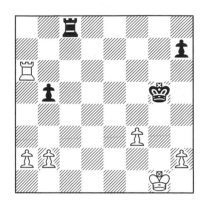

Diagram 11
Position after 27...Kh6

Diagram 12
Position after 32 Rxa6

The queens might have left the arena but Black isn't out of the woods by any means as White continues to enjoy an initiative. Both bishops are under fire, and the obvious 28 Bf7 Rb8 29 Kf2 isn't as dominating as it looks, e.g. 29...Rhc8 30 Rdd7 Rxc7 31 Rxc7 Bc8 32 Bd5 Bf5 33 Rc6 Rd8 etc.

28 Rd6

This doesn't so much protect the bishop as activate the rook.

28...Bc8!

Black has remained practical throughout. This time he avoids the problems that would beset him after 28...Bxf3 29 Bf7 (threatening Bxe8 as well as Rxf6+ and Rxf3) and 28...Rb8 29 Kf2, opting instead to take his chances in an ending where, for the price of a pawn, he can finally enjoy some activity.

29 Bxc8

29 Bd5 Rd8! 30 Rxf6+ Kg5 31 Rfc6 Rxd5 32 Rxc8 Rxc8 33 Rxc8 Rd2, but 29 Bf7!? might be worth a try, e.g. 29...Re2 30 f4 Rf8 31 Rxf6+ Kg7 32 Bh5+ Kxf6 33 Bxe2 or 29...Rd8 30 Rxf6+ Kg5 31 Rfc6 Kf4 32 Bb3, this second line looking okay for Black.

29...Rxc8 30 Rxf6+ Kg5 31 Rxc8 Rxc8 32 Rxa6 (Diagram 12)

All rook endings are drawn – apart from those that are lost. In this case Black's two pawn deficit is irrelevant as both his king and rook are active. Black's determination thus far has resulted in a psychologically boosting role reversal as White has had to adjust to defending since cashing in his lead. Now 32...Kf4!? 33 Rf6+ Ke3 34 b4 Rc2 35 a3 Ra2 transposes to the game, but 34 Kg2 Rc2+ 35 Kg3 Rxb2 36 Re6+ Kd3 37 Rb6 Kc4 38 Ra6 gives White something to bite on. A better try for Black would be 32...Rc1+ 33 Kf2 Rc2+ 34 Kg3 Rxb2 35 h4+ Kf5, when the king stands in front of the passed pawn.

32...Rc2!

This is even stronger, for the moment keeping White's king on the back rank.

33 b4 Kf4 34 Rf6+ Ke3 35 a3 Ra2 36 Rf5 Rxa3 37 Kg2 Rb3 38 Re5+

Of course we have to look at what happens to White's b-pawn after 38 Rxb5 Kf4 39 Rb8 Rb2+ 40 Kh3 Kxf3 41 b5 Ke4 42 Kg3 Kd5 43 h4 (Diagram 13)

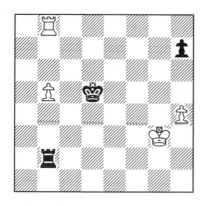

Diagram 13
Position after 43 h4

Diagram 14
Position after 56...Rd1+

Imagine getting this far after surviving the long journey since the initial 20 Nxe6 and then deciding what to do next now that the draw is so near. In fact 43...Kc5?? – however natural looking – loses: 44 Kg4 Rg2+ 45 Kh5 Rg7 46 b6 Kc6 47 Kh6 Re7 48 h5 Re5 49 Rh8 Kxb6 50 Rxh7 Re6+ 51 Kg7 Kc5 52 Kf8! Kd4 53 Rd7+ Ke5 54 Kg7 Kf5 55 Rd5+ Ke4 56 Ra5 etc. But 43...Rb4! (Cifuentes) saves the day: 44 h5 h6! 45 Rb6 (45 b6 Kc5) 45...Ke5 and Black's king is near enough.

38...Kf4 39 Re4+ Kf5 40 Kg3 Rb2 41 Rh4 Kf6 42 h3

White is defending everything, but this won't win the game.

42...Rb3 43 Rf4+ Kg6 44 Rd4 Rb1 45 Kh4

After 45 Kf4 Kf6 Black holds his ground.

45...Kf6 46 Kg4 Ke5 47 Re4+ Kf6 48 Rd4 Ke5 49 Re4+ Kf6 50 Rf4+ Kg6 51 Rd4 h5+ 52 Kg3 Kf7 53 Kf4 Kf6 54 Ke3 Ke5 55 f4+

55 Rh4 Rb3+ 56 Ke2 Kf6 gets White nowhere.

55...Ke6 56 Kd3 Rd1+ (Diagram 14) 57 Kc3 Rc1+ 58 Kd2 Rb1 59 Ke3 Re1+ 60 Kd2 Rf1 ½-½

A marathon defensive display from Lautier. White had a chance or two to make more of his attack but Black refused to bend and made put up a fight right up to the ending.

Drawn Endings Need to be Drawn

This is fairly obvious, of course, but thanks to the ever-accelerating time limits we have to put up these days, many of us succeed in messing up these situations, no matter how simple they might appear. The following example is typical in that it seems to present the defender with the easiest of tasks yet – right until the end – requires careful defence.

□ **M.Vershinin** ■ **L.Voloshin**

Litomysl 1995

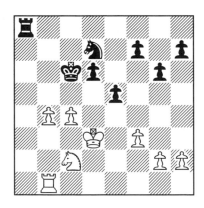

Diagram 15	Diagram 16
Position after 33 Nc2	Position after 39 Kd2!

White has just dropped his knight back from e3 to c2 in order to contest the a-file and effectively force the trade of rooks (and in doing so edge closer to the draw). If Black is to make a stab at an advantage he must try now.

33...d5 34 cxd5+ Kxd5 35 Ra1 Rxa1 36 Nxa1 f5

Passed pawns are important in endings but so is territory, and here the b-pawn has no chance of getting anywhere and serves only as a distraction. Meanwhile Black's pawn mass holds more potential, while his more advanced king is another factor. We could say that all this is academic as the ending is drawn, but we should make a habit of approaching such endings with extreme care.

 WARNING: Never relax when 'playing out' a drawn ending – anything less than 100% effort and attention merely increases the opposition's winning chances, and every half-point counts.

37 Nb3 Nf6 38 Nc5 Kd6

Black intends ...Nd5 to hit the b-pawn and toy with ...Nf4(+).

39 Kd2! (Diagram 16)

This is the kind of move that does need proper analysis, White responding to Black's crafty retreat with a practical one of his own, making way for Nd3.

39...Nd5 40 Nd3 e4

40...g5!? makes sense as it maintains the tension and steps up the pressure a little, whereas the text simplifies prematurely.

41 fxe4 fxe4 42 Nc5 e3+ 43 Ke2 Nxb4 44 Ne4+ Ke5 45 Kxe3 (Diagram 17)

Diagram 17
Position after 45 Kxe3

Diagram 18
Position after 54...hxg5 mate

Now we are reduced to just two pawns each, and on the same side, too. Most of the time a draw could be agreed here, but Black carries on because he has a few checks coming.

45...Nc2+ 46 Kf3

46 Kd3 Ne1+ drops the g2-pawn.

46...Nd4+

46...Ne1+ 47 Kf2 Nxg2 doesn't win a pawn because White has 48 Ng5, when 48...Nf4 49 Nxh7 Ne6 sees White's knight trapped yet perfectly safe.

47 Ke3 Nf5+ 48 Kf3

48 Kd3 is possible, but White does better to keep his king around the action area. (You might think that 'action' just isn't the appropriate word here, but there are still a couple of nasty banana skins that White needs to avoid).

48...Nh4+ 49 Kg3 Kxe4 50 Kxh4 Kf4

The draw edges closer and closer. Should they shake hands now? What would you play now?

51 g3+!

This is, in fact, the only move. The harmless looking 51 g4, for example, walks into trouble after 51...h6 52 g5 (52 h3 h5) 52...h5 and White must part with the g-pawn. The same happens in the event of 51 h3 h6 52 g4 h5 53 g5 (53 gxh5 g5 mate) 53...Kf5 etc. And for those of you who thought the draw was trivial, here's a funny but very realistic line: 52 g3+ Kf3! 53 g4 Kf4 54 g5 hxg5 mate **(Diagram 18)**.

Hopefully this position will serve to remind us that it is imperative not to relax in endings, however trivial the defensive task might seem (this game, for instance, couldn't have appeared more trivial).)

51...Kf3 52 Kg5 Kg2 53 h4 Kh3 54 h5 ½-½

Every now and then we are fortunate enough to be involved in a fiery battle in which we are faced with numerous difficult decisions. The adrenaline rush is such that losing this type of game might not seem as disappointing as would normally be the case. This is natural, but of course the kind of attitude that, over time, can make us a little bit too relaxed when these episodes come around and, consequently, perhaps prevent us from putting in maximum effort. The pundits say of nerve-jangling soccer matches that a draw is a 'fair' result, and the same can be said of competitive chess. Here is an entertaining, instructive example:

☐ **C.Lutz** ■ **B.Gelfand**

Dortmund Candidates 2002

1 e4 c5 2 Nf3 d6 3 d4 cxd4 4 Nxd4 Nf6 5 Nc3 a6 6 Bg5 e6 7 f4

Given the subject matter of this book, we don't want to get bogged down with (and distracted by) the latest trends of opening theory here, suffice to say that we are in for a complex line of the Sicilian in which prisoners tend not to be taken.

7...Nbd7 8 Qf3 Qc7 9 0-0-0

I think we already have a pretty good idea of the kind of game White has in mind, with more space and a big lead in (menacing) development. But the Sicilian is a cagey, dangerous animal and one that is likely to bite back at any time.

9...b5 10 Bxb5 (Diagram 19)

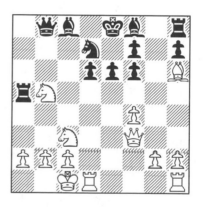

Diagram 19
Position after 10 Bxb5

Diagram 20
Position after 14 Bh6!?

Here we go. Black has only three pieces out so White strikes. Notice that this will mean gifting Black ready-made open files down which a counter could be launched against White's king, but you can't make an omelette without breaking eggs.

10...axb5 11 Ndxb5 Qb8 12 e5

We've barely played a dozen moves and the temperature is really hotting up. Apart from exf6 White also threatens Qxa8, when recapture meets with the fork on c7. For the moment we should put ourselves in Black's shoes and try to see how we would deal with the early attack.

12...Ra5

This is an unorthodox looking defence that I would expect to see at the higher and lower levels while, in-between, 12...Bb7 would probably be the choice. After 13 Qe2 dxe5 14 Qc4 Be7 15 Nc7+ Kf8 16 Rxd7 Nxd7 17 Rd1 Bxg5 18 fxg5 Bc8 19 N3b5 g6 the situation was unclear in E.Kengis-S.Dvoirys, USSR 1982. A decade later White opted for 17 Bxe7+!? Kxe7 18 Rd1 in J.Van der Wiel-O.Renet, Cannes 1992. There followed 18...Bd5 19 N3xd5+ exd5 20 Nxd5+ Kd8 (20...Kf8? 21 Nc7) 21 Nb4 Qc7 22 Qxf7 Ra5 23 Nd5 Rxd5 24 Rxd5 Re8 25 Qxg7 and the pawns had an edge over the knight.

13 exf6 gxf6 14 Bh6!? (Diagram 20)

By now we should not be surprised to see this kind of uncompromising sacrifice. Experience is a factor in finding these moves when analysing the possibilities at the board, and for those of you whose opening repertoire features pet lines that are prone to producing complex, cut-throat positions, it pays to play through relevant quality games in order to get acquainted with any squares or pawns that might tend to come under the microscope.

 WARNING: Beware enemy pieces that can flush out your key defenders from crucial posts.

14...Bxh6 15 Nxd6+

It is important to keep the momentum going in situations where both sides are threatening, so White makes sure to make his presence felt.

15...Ke7 16 Kb1

This does place the king on the b-file, but White wants to be able to move his knight from d6 without having to deal with a check on f4, and the pin on the f4-pawn also would have given Black the chance to hit back with ...Ne5.

16...Rd8

L.Psakhis-Y.Anikaev, Frunze 1979 went 16...Nb6 17 Nce4!? Na4? 18 Nxc8+ Rxc8 19 Qa3+! Nc5 (19...Ke8?? 20 Nxf6 mate) 20 Qxa5 Nxe4 21 Qa3+ Nc5 22 g3 with a clear advantage to White. 17...Nd5 is a big improvement, when 18 c4 is well balanced, although Black is the one on the back foot. However, despite the fact that Black seems to be assigned the role of defender in these lines the game is fluid enough for the roles to change at any time.

17 Rhe1

White's final piece comes into play.

17...Nb6 18 Ncb5 (Diagram 21)

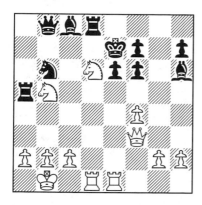

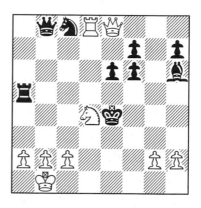

Diagram 21
Position after 18 Ncb5

Diagram 22
Position after 25...Ke4

It is fair to say that White has sufficient compensation, with a couple of pawns for the piece and his entire army participating in piling on the pressure. But Black – apart from the potentially useful extra piece – has the bishop pair and a presence on the queenside that White can ill afford to under-estimate. In other words the makings of an interesting finale. The text closes out Black's rook along the rank and thus makes Nf5+ a genuine possibility. How would you react?

18...Ba6

18...Rd7 19 Qc6 Kf8 20 Nxc8 Rxd1+ 21 Rxd1 Nxc8 22 Rd8+ Kg7 23 Qe8 is given by Tyomkin. It looks like Black's days are numbered but in fact a clean finish is by no means clear, e.g. 23...Kg6 (23...Bxf4 24 Qh8+ Kg6 25 g4!) 24 f5+ Kxf5! (24...exf5 25 Qg8+ Bg7 26 Rd7) 25 Nd4+ Ke4 **(Diagram 22)**.

Nevertheless, I'm not sure that I'd want to be in Black's shoes here. After 26 Qxf7 it would appear that Black's king is not made of steel, e.g. 26...Qb6 27 Qxf6! Rf5 28 Qh4+ Bf4 (28...Ke5 29 Nc6+! Qxc6 30 Qd4 mate) 29 Qe1+ Be3 30 Nxf5 Qxd8 31 Nxe3, or 26...Qf4 27 Qxe6+ Re5 (27...Qe5 28 Qc4) 28 Qc6+ Ke3 29 Nf3 Kf2 30 Rd1 etc.

18...Rxb5 is no less interesting: 19 Nxb5 and now 19...Nc4 20 Qb3 Nd2+

21 Rxd2 Rxd2 22 Qb4+ Rd6 (22...Ke8 23 Qxd2 Qxb5 24 Qc3) 23 g3 Bd7
24 Qxd6+ Qxd6 was agreed drawn in M.Brodsky-G.Timoshchenko,
Moscow 1992. After 25 Nxd6 Kxd6 26 b4 e5 Black comes out fighting,
but the queenside pawns look intimidating. The alternative 19...Rxd1+
also leads quickly to an ending in the event of 20 Rxd1 Bxf4 21 g3 Be5
22 Qa3+ Ke8 23 Nd6+ Bxd6 24 Qxd6 Qxd6 25 Rxd6 Nd5 26 c4 (Diagram 23)

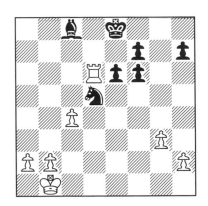
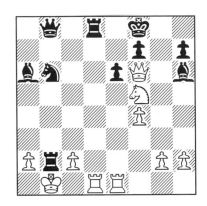

Diagram 23
Position after 26 c4

Diagram 24
Position after 21...Rxb2+!

Endings with rook against two pieces are notoriously difficult to evalu-
ate during play because various factors have different implications
from game to game. Here the three passed pawns are White's collective
trump card. Then 26...Ne3 sends the knight too far from the destina-
tion of White's queenside pawns: 27 c5 Nf1 28 b4 Nxh2 29 b5 and the
pawns are very dangerous, or 27...Ke7 28 b4 e5 29 a4 Nf1 30 a5 etc.
Meanwhile 26...Ne7 27 b4 Nf5 28 Rb6 Ne3 29 b5 Nxc4 30 Rc6 Nd2+ 31
Kc1 Bd7 32 Rc7 again spells trouble for Black.

19 Nf5+

This was a new move at the time of the game (it should come as no
surprise nowadays that all this had been played before). 19 Qc3?
worked out well for Black in B.Kantsler-V.Kuporosov, Sochi 1979:
19...Rxb5! 20 Nxb5 Bxb5 21 Qb4+ Rd6 22 Qxb5 Bxf4 and Black stood
better. This thin line between success and failure is obviously a difficult
one to walk, both players needing to find a balance between attack and
defence. Indeed after the check Black has a 50-50 choice consisting of a
good and bad retreat of the king. Which is which?

19...Kf8!

This is the good one. For those of you who thought it made no difference whether the king dropped back to e8 or f8 because 19...Ke8 20 Qc6+ Kf8 21 Qc3 takes us to the main game, here's why your wrong: 20 Rxe6+!, when 20...fxe6 21 Qh5+ Kf8 22 Qxh6+ Ke8 23 Nfd6+ Rxd6 (23...Kd7 24 Qxh7+ Kc6 25 Na7+) 24 Nxd6+ Kd7 25 Ne4+ Kc6 26 Qxf6 leaves White way ahead, or 20...Kf8 21 Rxd8+ Qxd8 22 Rxb6! Bxb5 (22...Qxb6 23 Qa8+) 23 Rd6, which is even worse for Black.

20 Qc3! Rxb5

After 20...exf5? 21 Qxf6 White hits d8 and threatens Qh8, 21...Rxd1+ 22 Rxd1 Bxf4 23 Rd8+ Qxd8 24 Qxd8+ Kg7 25 Qd4+ f6 26 Qxb6 Rxb5 (26...Bd2 27 Nd4) 27 Qxa6 being decisive.

21 Qxf6 Rxb2+! (Diagram 24)

Finding this saver is no easy task, while finding it and working out that it is sound during the complications (and their implications) is another matter entirely.

TIP: As you're wading through the complexities of the opposition's numerous aggressive possibilities in a prolonged pressure situation, keep an eye out for disruptive sacrifices around the enemy king.

21...Rxd1+ 22 Rxd1 Rxf5 23 Qh8+ Ke7 24 Qxb8 and Black will lose more material.

22 Qxb2

White should accept immediately (and not with the king!) as 22 Ka1 Rxa2+ 23 Kxa2 Bc4+ leaves the king too exposed.

22...Nd5

Closing the d-file (shutting out White) and clearing the b-file (letting in Black).

23 Rxd5! (Diagram 25)

Not 23 Nxh6? Nc3+ or 23 Qxb8? Rxb8+ 24 Ka1 Bxf4 etc.

23...Qxb2+ 24 Kxb2 Bg7+!

A nice touch! I won't say why yet... 24...Rxd5 25 Nxh6 Rd2 26 g3 Rxh2 27 Ng4 Rh3 followed by ...h7-h5 offers Black some chances in the ending but White's queenside pawns remain a danger. The text is far more uncompromising.

25 Nxg7 Rxd5

This way – forcing the capture to be made on g7 – leaves the knight trapped.

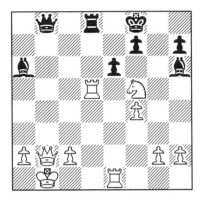

Diagram 25	Diagram 26
Position after 23 Rxd5!	Position after 27 Rxe6

26 Nxe6+ fxe6 27 Rxe6 ½-½ (Diagram 26)

A draw does indeed seem like a fair result after so much action and entertainment. White has four pawns for the bishop but 27...Bf1! (Tyomkin) makes room for the rook so that after 28 g3 Black has 28...Rb5+ 29 Kc3 Rc5+, 30 Kd2 allowing 30...Bc4, picking up the a-pawn.

Chapter Six

Provocation

Introduction

There is something to be said for playing provocatively and actively inviting the opposition to come out fighting. They might attack prematurely, in which case you will be happy to oblige, putting up with any inconvenience in order to mop up and emerge well ahead. Your opponent might be too loose and aggressive, or too passive and not used to attacking (and therefore like a fish out of water if it seems that aggression is his only policy). If you're happy to risk being attacked then this strategy pays, as you either succeed in taking liberties or find yourself in the desired fight. Note that provocation can be particularly effective with White because, apart from the advantage of the first move that Black doesn't enjoy when goading his opponent, the psychological implications when Black is invited to assume the role of the aggressor are worth investigating for those of you whose pre-tournament preparation involves trying to unlock the minds of prospective opponents.

☐ **M.Makarov** ■ **K.Sakaev**

Russian Team Championship 2002

We join the game after the once very trendy variation that runs:

1 d4 Nf6 2 c4 e6 3 Nf3 d5 4 Nc3 c6 5 e3 Nbd7 6 Qc2 Bd6 7 g4 Bb4 8 Bd3?! dxc4 9 Bxc4 b5!? 10 Be2 (Diagram 1)

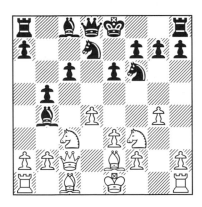

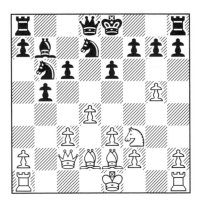

Diagram 1
Position after 10 Be2

Diagram 2
Position after 13...N5b6!?

Clearly the g-pawn has been dangled in front of Black in order to invite the opening of the g-file after ...Nxg4, Rg1 with the idea that White's king can go west whereas Black's might be more problematic. Here, still, Black is allowed to take on g4, but Sakaev instead ignores the g-pawn. In fact he ignores the kingside altogether, practically waving White forward by calmly concentrating on the other flank.

10...Bb7 11 g5

11 Bd2 is another possibility, but White pushes on – as would most players.

11...Nd5 12 Bd2 Bxc3 13 bxc3 N5b6!? (Diagram 2)

What is Black doing? Having been evicted from the traditional outpost on f6 the knight voluntarily travels further away from where White clearly intends to focus. As we shall see, Black's strategy is put in place with precisely this in mind.

14 Rg1 Rc8 15 Rg3 a6 16 Qe4 (Diagram 3)

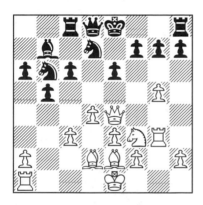

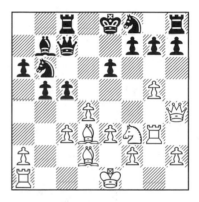

Diagram 3	Diagram 4
Position after 16 Qe4	Position after 18...c5

Pinning the c6-pawn to the bishop en route to the kingside. With so many pieces huddled up on the queenside most players would be starting – if they hadn't already – to worry about White's build-up, but White's unsubtle show of aggression is a key part of Black's strategy.

16...Qc7

Coming to the aid of the bishop.

17 Qh4

Apart from having a menacing air, the queen transfer introduces the threat of g5-g6 in view of the pin on the h-file.

17...Nf8!

A key move. The knight covers g6, but there is much more to this ostensibly defensive retreat than meets the eye. We are about to see another example of the knight's flexibility.

18 Bd3 c5 (Diagram 4)

The thrust upon which Black's play is based. Nothing in particular is attacked (although now we see some of the logic behind Rg3) but unleashing the bishop is significant indeed. Moreover, taking a closer look at the position we see that from a structural point of view Black is doing much better. White, meanwhile, is on a one-way course to a kingside offensive.

19 Ne5 Nbd7 20 Nxd7

The immediate 20 f4 looks better.

20...Qxd7 21 Qg4

The next part of White's plan is to launch the kingside pawns.

21...Ng6 22 f4 Ne7 23 h4

Here they come...

23...Nf5 (Diagram 5)

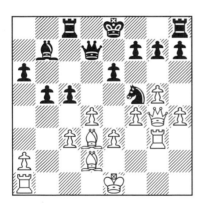

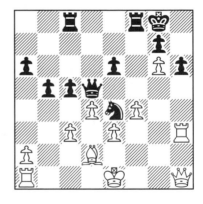

Diagram 5
Position after 23...Nf5

Diagram 6
Position after 30...0-0

The legion of pawns is well supported by heavy artillery but the nimble knight helps render their offensive useless. The voyage from d7 will continue as Black prepares to exploit the vulnerability of the hole on e4.

Note how poor White's bishop is on d2, and in turn the contrasting scopes of the remaining minor pieces in the event of 24 Bxf5 exf5, when White would be struggling to survive.

 TIP: When the opposition executes or prepares a pawn storm, keep an eye on any resulting weak squares created in enemy territory.

24 Rh3 Nd6 25 h5 Be4!

A hole is one thing, but when the positional price of over-eager attacking play is a hole in the middle of the board the aggressor can easily fall foul of his own recklessness.

26 Bxe4 Nxe4 27 Qg2 Qd5

Black has not yet undertaken any offensive play himself, but his centralised, dominating pieces and far superior pawn structure combine to form a near decisive advantage.

28 g6

White has come this far and might as well continue, and the alternative is to sit and wait for his numerous weaknesses to be fully exposed.

28...fxg6 29 hxg6 h6 30 Qh1 0-0 (Diagram 6)

It's always nice to castle when your opponent has gone to such great lengths to crash through your defences. Ironically it is White who now needs to find somewhere for his own king. Chigorin would be proud of Black's play, even if the contributing factor in arriving at this excellent position has been White's rather blinkered, unsubtle approach. A successful attack tends to need sufficient fire-power with which to force the issue, and this is clearly not the case as far as White is concerned.

31 Rxh6?!

31 Rh5 Rf5 will take longer for Black to cash in (...c5xd4 looms). The text is a token show of aggression before the role-reversal is complete.

31...gxh6 32 Qxh6 Rc7 33 0-0-0 Nf2

33...Qxa2 is simple and very strong (Black is a rook up, after all), so perhaps Black was short of time around here. The game ended:

34 Rg1 Rg7 35 Be1 Nd3+ 36 Kd2 Nxe1 37 Kxe1 Qe4 38 Kf2 cxd4 39 cxd4 0-1

Taking the Bait

A common chess conundrum is whether or not to help ourselves to a free pawn (usually one that is deliberately put on offer by the opposition) when doing so opens up a line of attack against our king position. Often there is a certain amount of bluffing going on, as the aggressor might be trying to gain time by hoping to get away with it, while being prepared to attack a pawn down if the bluff is called (a semi-bluff). The problem facing the defender in this situation is that not taking the pawn can result in more inconvenience than biting the bullet, so I would suggest that players properly investigate the consequences of accepting such gifts. After all, if the opposition's desired/threatened initiative fails to offer sufficient compensation, then the extra pawn will come in very handy. Here is a typical example:

□ **V.Rajlich** ■ **G.Antal**

Budapest 2002

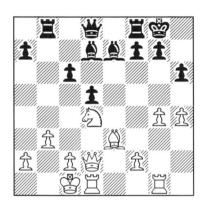 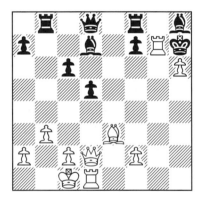

Diagram 7	Diagram 8
Position after 16 b3	Position after 21 Rg7+!

White's offensive is the more developed thanks to the advanced pawns, but Black, to move, has the option of picking off the h4-pawn. This would displace the bishop and most likely give White an open line on which to attack, but Black is confident in his defensive resources...

16...Bxh4! 17 Nf5

Less troublesome for Black is 17 g5 hxg5 18 Bxg5 Bxg5 19 Rxg5, when 19...f6 20 Rh5 seems to give White enough play for the pawn, but

19...g6 20 Rdg1 Qf6 probably doesn't. The text is aimed at opening the h-file instead.

17...Bg5

17...Bxf5 18 gxf5 Kh7 19 Bxa7 Ra8 20 Bd4 Bf6 21 a4 favours White. 17...Bf6 looks the most natural retreat, but then Black has to deal with 18 Nxh6+ gxh6 19 g5, e.g. 19...Bh8 20 gxh6+ Kh7 21 Rg7+! **(Diagram 8)** 21...Bxg7 22 hxg7 and now 22...Rg8 23 Rh1+ Kg6 (23...Kxg7 24 Bb6!) 24 Qe2 leaves the king too exposed (try a few lines out and you'll see what I mean), while 22...Re8 23 Rh1+ Kg8 (23...Kxg7 24 Rg1+ wins for White) 24 Bb6 (remember to keep your eyes peeled for these standard, tempo-gaining clearance devices) 24...Re1+ 25 Qxe1 Qf6 (25...axb6 26 Qg1) 26 Bxa7 is very good for White.

18 Bxg5

I prefer 18 f4 Bf6 19 g5 hxg5 20 fxg5 Be5 21 Bd4, but White wants that h-file.

18...hxg5

Not 18...Qxg5?? 19 Qxg5 hxg5 20 Ne7+ Kh7 21 Rh1 mate.

19 Rg3 Re8 20 Rh1 Qf6 21 Kb1 g6 (Diagram 9)

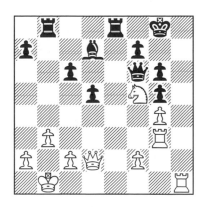

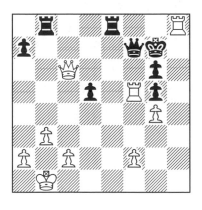

Diagram 9	**Diagram 10**
Position after 21...g6	Position after 31 Rxf5

This is what White was looking for, but it would appear that the game is drifting away from him (hindsight is a useful analytical tool).

22 Nh6+

White has a specific idea in mind. Otherwise he might have considered

22 Rh6, when 22...Re4 23 Rgh3 Rbe8 24 Rh8+ Qxh8 25 Rxh8+ Kxh8 26 Nd6 Re1+ 27 Kb2 R8e2 28 Qd4+ Kg8 29 Qxa7 Re7 is not clear, but 22...Bxf5 23 gxf5 Qxf5 24 Rxg5 Re1+! 25 Qxe1 (25 Kb2 Qf6+ 26 c3 Qe7) 25...Qxg5 sees Black emerge with his extra pawn intact.

22...Kg7 23 Nxf7?!

After 23 Rgh3 d4 White is sitting pretty with nowhere to go, but the text is one of those sacrifices that is not as effective as it looks (assuming you think it looks effective).

23...Kxf7

23...Qxf7? fully justifies White's attack: 24 Qd4+ Kf8 25 Rh8+ Ke7 26 Qe5+ Be6 (26...Qe6 27 Rh7+ Kd8 28 Qxb8+) 27 Qc7+ Bd7 28 Re3+ Kf6 29 Rf3+ Bf5 30 Qxc6+ Kg7 31 Rxf5 **(Diagram 10)**.

Perhaps this is the line that inspired White to go down this path. Now 31...Rxh8 32 Rxf7+ Kxf7 33 Qxd5+ is a very poor ending for Black, while 31...Qxf5 32 gxf5 Kxh8 33 Qf6+ Kg8 34 Qxg6+ Kf8 35 f6 Rb7 36 Qh6+ Kg8 37 Qxg5+ Kf8 38 Qxd5 is even worse.

24 Rh7+ Ke6

The king has been forced out into the open, but exploiting this at the cost of a piece is by no means guaranteed.

 TIP: Many attacks fail because the aggressor overestimates his chances by not properly evaluating the situation that arises immediately after a sacrifice.

25 c4 Kd6 26 c5+ (Diagram 11)

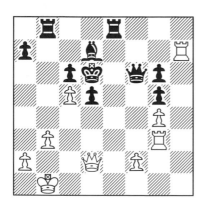

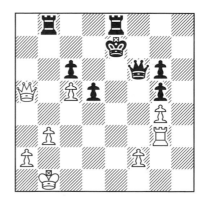

Diagram 11
Position after 26 c5+

Diagram 12
Position after 31...Ke7

After the alternative 26 cxd5 cxd5 27 Rd3 Re5 28 Qa5 Qf4 Black both holds and creates threats of his own.

26...Kc7

There is no reason to play 26...Kxc5? 27 Rxd7 as Black is not afraid of the coming queen intrusion.

27 Qa5+ Kc8

White looks threatening, but that's as good as it gets.

28 Rxd7

Having reached the end of the line as far as a successful attack is concerned, White has a futile flurry of checks. 28 Qa6+ Rb7 29 Rxd7 Re1+ 30 Kc2 Qxf2+ and White gets mated.

28...Kxd7 29 Qxa7+ Kc8 30 Qa6+ Kd8 31 Qa5+ Ke7 (Diagram 12)

The king heads back to whence it came. White is simply a rook down and resigned a few moves later. Note how quickly White's game fell apart – all thanks to over-ambitious, albeit tempting sacrificial play.

There is a difference between deliberately playing openings and defences that naturally induce attacking play from the opposition, and choosing a repertoire that presents both sides with attacking chances and therefore tempts the opponent into promising looking but ultimately dubious offensive forays. The Sicilian Defence is perhaps the best such example, the main lines producing complex scenarios in which victory can often come about as a result of soaking up pressure in the face of an unsound attack. Of course not all players are comfortable adopting this kind of strategy, but it is worth investigating and, ironically, should be part of the natural attacking player's armoury.

□ A.Motylev ■ M.Makarov
Russian Team Championship 2002

1 e4 c5 2 Nf3 d6 3 d4 cxd4 4 Nxd4 Nf6 5 Nc3 a6 6 f3 e5 7 Nb3 Be6 8 Be3 Nbd7 9 g4 b5 10 g5 b4 11 Ne2 Nh5 12 Qd2 a5 13 Ng3 Nxg3 14 hxg3 a4 15 Nc1 Qa5 16 f4 (Diagram 13)

We begin at the critical point. White has been busy on the kingside, with Black wasting no time countering on the queenside – typical Sicilian fare, as is the fact that neither player has bothered to address king safety. Here Black had been doing okay with 16...g6!, e.g. 17 Nd3 Bg7

18 a3 bxa3 19 Qxa5 Rxa5 20 Rxa3 0-0 21 Bg2 Rc8 22 Kd2 exf4 23 gxf4 Rb5 24 Rb1 Nb6 25 Bxb6 Rxb6 26 Bf3 h6 and the dark-squared bishop guaranteed Black sufficient play in F.Nijboer-E.L'Ami, Dieren 2002. Instead Makarov prefers to exploit White's apparently slow development by opening up the centre and embarking on an energetic assault on the queenside.

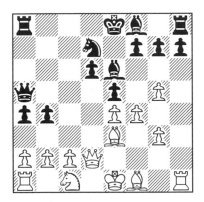

Diagram 13
Position after 16 f4

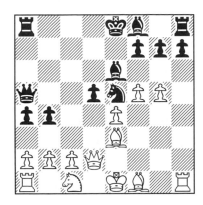

Diagram 14
Position after 18...Ne5

16...exf4?! 17 gxf4 d5 18 f5 Ne5 (Diagram 14)

This activation of the knight is the point behind Black's flurry in the centre. After the sensible looking 19 Be2 Bd7 20 exd5 Bxf5 or 20 Qxd5 Qxd5 21 exd5 Ra5!? Black is doing fine, so White 'allows' Black his fun on the queenside.

19 Qf2 b3+

Having 'forced' the removal of the queen from d2 Black ploughs on. White did well in E.Rodriguez Guerrero-I.Herrera, Mancha Real 2002 after 19...Ng4 20 Qf4 Nxe3 21 fxe6! Qa7 22 exf7+ Kd8 23 g6! Nxc2+ 24 Kd2 b3 (24...Nxa1 25 Rxh7) 25 Nd3 h6 26 Rh5.

20 Bd2

20 c3 Ng4 21 Qf4 Nxe3 22 Qxe3 looks clearly better for White but the text falls in with Black's (unsound) plan.

20...Bb4 21 c3

Not 21 fxe6? Bxd2+ when White is in trouble as recapturing on d2 allows the deadly fork on f3. Note that this is the kind of finish that lures players into juicy looking tactical sequences.

21...a3 (Diagram 15)

In the event of 21...Bc5 White must avoid 22 Qg3 dxe4 23 fxe6 Nf3+ 24 Ke2 0-0-0 with a great position for Black, but Ftacnik's 22 Qg2 Bd7 (22...dxe4 23 Qxe4) 23 axb3 dxe4 24 b4 is clearly favourable for White. Incidentally I had a look at what happens if White meets 21...Bc5 with the obvious 22 Qf4 here, and even after 22...Bd6 23 fxe6 Nd3+ 24 Bxd3 Bxf4 (again acquiescing to what would be Black's 'desired' continuation following ...Bc5) White emerges well on top with 25 exf7+ Kxf7 26 Rf1, e.g. 26...bxa2 27 Nxa2 Rhf8 28 Bxf4 Kg8 29 0-0-0 etc.

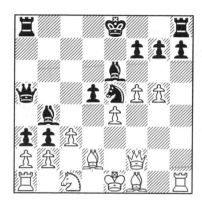

Diagram 15
Position after 21...a3

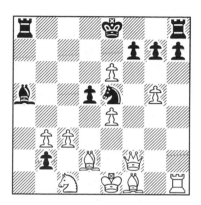

Diagram 16
Position after 24 fxe6

22 axb3

22 bxa3? Bc5 23 Qg3 b2 not only refuses to play along but also leaves White struggling to survive. But 22 cxb4 is possible, when 22...axb2 23 bxa5 bxa1Q 24 fxe6 0-0 (24...b2 25 exf7+ Nxf7 26 Bb5+ Ke7 27 Qc5+ and mate is unavoidable) 25 Qf5 g6 26 Qh3 h5 27 axb3 is decisive.

22...axb2

White also had to consider 22...Ng4 23 Qe2 axb2 24 Rxa5 Bxa5 25 fxe6 b1Q 26 Qb5+ Kf8 27 Bd3 Qa1 28 Qd7 fxe6 29 0-0+ with mate on the horizon.

23 Rxa5 Bxa5

23...Rxa5 24 cxb4 b1Q (24...Ra1 25 Qf4 Rxc1+ 26 Bxc1 b1Q 27 fxe6) 25 Qf4 Qxe4+ 26 Qxe4 dxe4 27 bxa5 is final.

24 fxe6 (Diagram 16)

Black is sure to get a second queen but all the excitement on the queenside has been at the cost of neglecting his king, which White can now concentrate on overpowering.

24...b1Q

The alternative is 24...fxe6 25 Bb5+ Kd8 26 Qc5!, when 26...b1Q 27 Qd6+ Kc8 28 Qxe6+ Kc7 29 Qxe5+ Kb6 30 Qd6+ Kxb5 31 Qxd5+ Ka6 32 Qc6+ Bb6 33 Be3 Rab8 34 0-0 is a nice pre-finishing touch, but 31 c4+! dxc4 32 bxc4+ Ka4 (32...Kxc4 33 Qd5 mate) 33 Qd7+ Ka3 34 Rh3+ is quicker.

25 Bb5+ Kf8

Unfortunately for Black after 25...Kd8 White doesn't have to play the sensible 26 0-0 Qxe4 27 exf7 Rf8 with chances for both sides as there is 26 e7+! Kxe7 27 Qc5+ Kd8 28 Qxd5+ Kc7 29 Qxe5+.

26 Qc5+ Kg8 27 Qxd5 1-0

A sample finale is 27...Nf3+ 28 Kf2 Rd8 29 exf7+ Kf8 30 Qc5+ Kxf7 31 g6+ and mate looms. Note that Black's attempt to dictate proceedings was more of an inspired decision rather than one based on concrete variations. This happens more often than we realise – at all levels – and we should be alert to possibilities that put us on the defensive in the conventional sense yet, practically, permit us to happily bounce off the ropes to mop up the point when the opposition's fun is over and the attack is spent.

Come and Get Me...

In our next example Black jumps at the chance to punish his opponent's 'passive' treatment of the opening, only to find himself in an embarrassing predicament where he has clearly bitten off more than he can chew.

☐ E.Dizdarevic ■ I.Smirin

Sarajevo 2002

White – who has just nudged his f-pawn forward – is poised to round up the d-pawn. What can Black find by way of compensation? Or is it possible for Black to launch an offensive by exploiting his extra space and development lead?

14...d3

Here we go (as per plan for White). Perhaps 14...Bf5!? is preferable, e.g.

15 Nxd4 Nxd4 16 Qxd4 Qxd4+ 17 Bxd4 Rad8 18 Be5 Rfe8 (Hazai) with some compensation for the pawn. Hazai continues 19 f4 Be4 20 Bxe4 Nxe4 21 Bxg7 Kxg7, which seems reasonable, while White also has 20 Nc3 Bxg2 21 Kxg2, e.g. 21...Ng4 22 Nd5 Nxe5 23 fxe5 Bxe5 24 Rae1 with a well placed knight. Black's choice in the game is completely different.

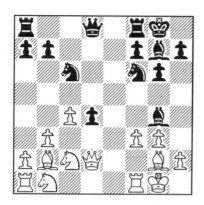

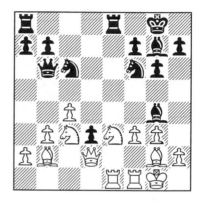

Diagram 17
Position after 14 f3

Diagram 18
Position after 17 Rae1

15 Ne3 Qb6

Black sets out his stall and begins a complex theme on pins. 15...Be6 16 Nc3 gives the game a different texture, where both sides have chances.

16 Nc3

Understandably White did not like the look of 16 fxg4?! Bh6! etc. The text keeps the threat to the bishop open while completing development and clamping down on d5 just in case a blockade becomes available.

16...Rfe8

The e3-knight gets a lot of attention in this game.

17 Rae1 (Diagram 18)

There is a great deal of tension in the diagram position. Black is clearly the more active and the d-pawn is both a strength and a weakness. It is not too late to settle for obvious compensation after 17...Be6 18 Qxd3 Rad8, when I prefer White in the long-term but there's still quite a way until the extra pawn means something. Instead Black justifies his opponent's come-and-get-me attitude and gets rather carried away with the energy in his set-up, throwing everything but the kitchen sink at the pin he's set up.

17...Bh6?

Come into my parlour, said the spider to the fly...

18 Ncd1!

It might seem that White is reduced to reacting to threats. Indeed he is, but now two of Black's pieces are under attack.

18...Nd4

Black now looks even more menacing, but he is lost. 18...Ne4 19 fxe4 Bxd1 is another try, when 20 Qf2 lifts the pin (preparing Nxd1), threatens mate in one and wins the game. White also had to take into account the entertaining 18...Rxe3 19 Nxe3 Re8 20 Bxf6 Bxe3+ (20...Rxe3 21 Kh1!) 21 Kh1 (Diagram 19)

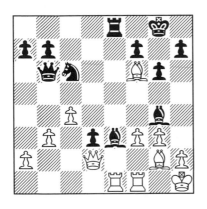

Diagram 19
Position after 21 Kh1

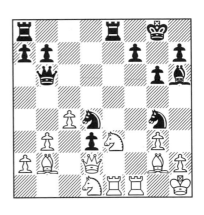

Diagram 20
Position after 20 Kh1

Why is it that so many of these flashy tactical sequences eventually come undone in the face of the very same theme upon which they are based? In this case Black finally wins control over e3, only to find himself on the wrong end of a deadly pin thanks to the back rank mate on e8.

 TIP: Watch out for threats from your opponent that leave him too vulnerable, then try to draw him in...

19 fxg4

Black has been sailing so dangerously close to the wind that something had to go, and his bishop had been hanging since we joined the game.

He can still play as if he has an initiative, but White has the extra piece and the decisive lead that came with it.

19...Nxg4 20 Kh1 (Diagram 20)

It was probably safe by now to just remove the d3-pawn, but by tucking the king away in the corner White at least does away with one of the pins. Meanwhile, in his efforts to win the game by pointing most of his forces directly at e3, Black has neglected the a1-h8 diagonal...

20...Nxe3

Also possible is 20...Nf5 21 c5! (taking the queen away from the defence of f6...) 21...Qxc5 (21...Qa6 22 Rxf5 gxf5 23 Qc3 f6 24 Nxf5) 22 Nxg4! Bxd2 23 Rxe8+ Rxe8 24 Nf6+ (Diagram 21)

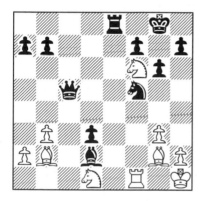

Diagram 21
Position after 24 Nf6+

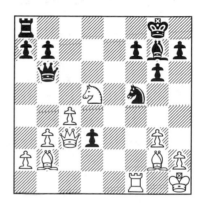

Diagram 22
Position after 24 Nd5!

White will win the queen back with interest.

21 Rxe3 Rxe3 22 Nxe3 Nf5

Black – only a piece down – seems to be finding ways of keeping the fire burning, and deserves some credit for seeing the theme through so far. However, all his effort is in vain, as the pin is effective only if it either ultimately wins material or keeps White tied up. Unfortunately for Black, neither is the case here.

23 Qc3

23 Rxf5 is another solution, e.g. 23...Bxe3 (23...gxf5 24 Qc3 f6 25 Bd5+ Kh8 26 Qxd3!) 24 c5! Bxd2 25 cxb6 gxf5 26 Bxb7 and if the rook moves White has bxa7 etc.

23...Bg7 24 Nd5! (Diagram 22)

White has gladly accepted the role as the player under pressure yet he is the one with the most powerful moves when the going gets tough. Just when Black appears to be making progress and a reward for his power-play is in sight, White comes over all uncompromising.

24...Bxc3 25 Nxb6 Bxb2 26 Nxa8 Ne3 27 Rf2 Bc3

Black cannot get his rook back with the d-pawn, and the game ended **28 Bf3 Be1 29 Rb2 g5 30 Nc7 g4 31 Nd5 Nxd5 32 Bxd5 1-0**

Inviting your opponent to come at you with all guns blazing because the offensive is unsound might be a good point earner but nevertheless requires careful, calm defence and the confidence to find the telling counter-punches when necessary. It might be best to try out this tactic against a certain type of player, while it obviously makes sense to have a good understanding of the opening in order to cope with whatever threats come your way.

WARNING: Even when provoking your opponent into carrying out an unsound attack is the best course, there is still a considerable risk element.

Although getting the king to 'safety' by castling early is one of the first things we learn, as we gain experience and begin to appreciate how such rules can be broken, other factors might take priority during the opening phase. Nevertheless, when leaving the king in the centre we must clearly be willing to face the occasional attempt from the opposition to land an early knockout blow. Moreover, the fact that such a sudden attack might not be sound doesn't mean that the road to refutation is an easy one. It is imperative that we feel comfortable (or, at least, not so uncomfortable that nerves have a negative, debilitating effect), confident that the predicament of an uncastled king is not one without resources. Some players, in fact, deliberately employ openings and defences in which delayed castling is a key feature, positively encouraging the opponent to punish their provocative play, thriving on the complexities and material imbalance that tend to be seen in these often brutal situations. I'm not advocating we all adopt such a strategy, merely suggesting that the reader find a collection of games similar to the next example in order to get a feel of what happens when the defender's king is sent packing. We will start at the beginning as Black's cheeky opening play sets the tone for what follows.

☐ **M.Marin** ■ **C.Ionescu**

Bucharest 1996

1 g3 c5 2 c4 Nf6 3 Bg2 e6 4 Nf3 a6 5 Nc3 b6 (Diagram 23)

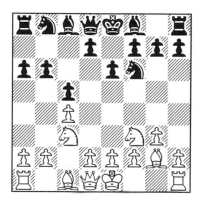

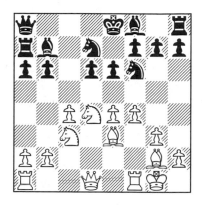

Diagram 23
Position after 5...b6

Diagram 24
Position after 11...Qa8

The theoretical rights and wrongs have no relevance for us as far as subject matter is concerned, suffice to say that Black would most likely emerge from the opening phase with a playable position should White choose to avoid hand-to-hand combat, Black's would-be Hedgehog set-up (characterised by the prickly employment of pawns on the third rank) popular at all levels of competition. Rather than shadow-box, Marin typically seeks to exploit his development advantage to generate an early initiative.

6 d4 cxd4 7 Nxd4 Ra7

I imagine that some of you would feel rather awkward in Black's position, while for others Ionescu's first eleven moves will prove inspirational...

8 0-0 Bb7

Of course this is a logical follow-up to ...a7-a6 and ...Ra7, but 8...Be7 is a sensible alternative, after which Black can avoid any funny stuff by simply castling before returning his attention to the queenside. The text continues an impressive looking mobilisation of the queenside forces.

9 e4

White would be doing himself no favours by trading bishops.

9...d6 10 Be3 Nbd7 11 f4

Not only is White close to completing development but he also enjoys a menacing space advantage.

11...Qa8 (Diagram 24)

It transpires that the diagram position is just what Black has been aiming for all along. Despite operating in confined quarters and posting the rook on a7 Black has succeeded in putting White's centre under pressure. The price is the kingside, which, during the build-up, seems to have been somewhat neglected.

12 f5 e5 13 Ne6!?

And this is what White has been waiting to unleash. A cheaper – albeit less ambitious – investment is 13 Nc2, when 13...Nxe4 14 Nd5 Bxd5 15 cxd5 Nef6 16 Nb4 a5 17 Nc6 Rc7 18 Rc1 Nc5 offers White obvious compensation in the shape of the advanced knight. But the text is a brutal attempt to catch the king unawares and hopefully without sufficient support from Black's forces, which don't appear to be ready for urgent defensive duty.

13...fxe6

Forced and best.

14 fxe6 Nc5

From here on in Black must be on his toes. The extra material in these situations is a dormant factor only, the outcome of the game balancing on the battle between attackers (fluid) and defenders (scattered, poorly posted). 14...Nb8? doesn't look quite right and in fact falls foul of 15 Rxf6! gxf6 16 Qh5+ Kd8 (16...Ke7 17 Qf7+) 17 Bxb6+ etc.

15 Rxf6

What attracts the more courageous players to this form of 'provocative defending' is the level of skill often required by the attacker. It is not too difficult a task for most players to see how an attack might be launched against an uncastled king, but maintaining the pressure through sacrifices is not as easy as the attacking guides suggest. The attacker often must be willing to follow one investment with another just to be able to maintain the pressure – difficult for most players from a psychological point of view as there is no immediate, concrete reward.

> **NOTE: Remember that the attacker, too, is under pressure to succeed.**

The text is the thematic, consistent follow-up, but 15 b4 also needs to be considered as it aims to clear the bishop's view of b6. Unlike Marin's forcing selection, hitting the knight is the kind of move that troubles defenders as it presents Black with a choice, in this case between ...Ncxe4 and ...Nxe6. The former sees the tension mount further: 15...Ncxe4 16 Nxe4 and then 16...Bxe4 17 Rxf6 gxf6 (17...Bxg2 18 Bxb6 Bh1 19 Rf2 Rb7 20 c5 keeps White in the driving seat) 18 Bxb6! (not 18 Qh5+? Bg6 19 Bxa8 Bxh5 20 Bc6+ Kd8 21 Bxb6+ Rc7) 18...Ke7 (18...Bxg2?? 19 Qh5+) 19 Bxe4 Qxe4 20 Bxa7 Kxe6 21 Qb3 and Black still has problems to solve regarding his king. Meanwhile, 16...Nxe4 17 Rf7 looks like a defender's nightmare, e.g. 17...Nc3 (17...Bc6 18 b5 axb5 19 cxb5 Rxa2 20 Rxa2 Qxa2 21 bxc6 Qxe6 22 Rb7) 18 Bxb7 Rxb7 19 Qh5! g6 20 Qf3 Ra7 21 Qf6 Rg8 22 Bg5 (Diagram 25)

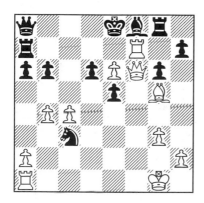

Diagram 25
Position after 22 Bg5

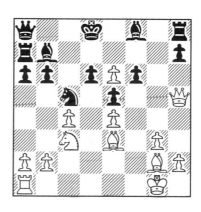

Diagram 26
Position after 16...Kd8

This position would be a case of provocation gone badly wrong, as Black's king is in serious trouble. A sample continuation is 22...b5 23 c5 Ne2+ 24 Kf2 Nc3 25 Rxa7 Ne4+ 26 Kg2 Nxf6+ 27 Rxa8+ Ke7 28 c6 etc.

Since the e6-pawn is such a useful member of White's team it makes sense to eliminate it, and after 15...Nxe6! 16 Bxb6 Bc6 17 Bxa7 Qxa7+ 18 Kh1 White's attack has come to an end and Black is doing fine with the two pieces for rook and pawn (the dark squares are a problem for White).

15...gxf6 16 Qh5+ Kd8 (Diagram 26)

Both players will have had this position in mind when Black was dancing around on the queenside. White has succeeded in displacing his opponent's king, while Black has taken a considerable material lead for the inconvenience. Note that Black's strange piece placement can be unsettling for the attacker, who must look out for defensive resources coming from unconventional places.

17 b4

Having invested a rook White has only the one gear left, and with the king arriving on d8 the weak point on b6 gains in significance. 17 Qf7?! jumps in but helps Black after 17...Be7 18 b4 Rf8 19 Qxh7 Nxe6, e.g. 20 Bxb6+ Ke8 21 Rd1 Bc6 and Black's forces are beginning to form a coherent defensive unit.

17...Bc6

With the texture of the game established Black sets about reorganising, rallying around the king. (Not 17...Nxe6?? 18 Qf7).

18 bxc5 bxc5 19 Rd1 Kc8 (Diagram 27)

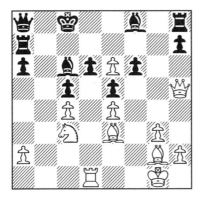

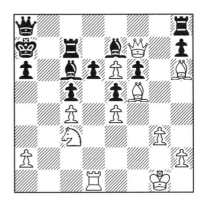

Diagram 27
Position after 19...Kc8

Diagram 28
Position after 23...Ka7

Black is now 'only' an exchange up, but does have solid centre pawns as protection, and the king looks a little healthier. White, for his part, no longer needs to go all-out for a knockout blow, and can instead combine his aggression with 'normal' play.

20 Bh3

The bishop was doing nothing on g2. After the immediate 20 Nd5?! Black can ignore the threat to the f6-pawn and instead come to life with 20...Qb7, e.g. 21 Nxf6 Be7 22 Nd7 Qb2, when the knight stands next to the king but in fact threatens nothing, while the queen's incursion means something.

20...Be7 21 Qf7 Rc7

The regrouping continues.

22 Bf5

White is seeking to exploit Black's apparent abandonment of the king-side, sending in the forces while Black is busy addressing his king's safety.

22...Kb7 23 Bh6 Ka7 (Diagram 28)

The journey has finally ended (Black does like this a7-square!), but has the quest been a worthwhile venture for Black? He remains an exchange up, has a reasonably solid looking set-up and his forces are ready to spring to life. On the other hand, White, with the superior pawn structure and more active pieces, can claim definite compensation. However, the psychological situation must be taken into consideration here. Black has been looking for a fight from the very beginning when he started messing around on the queenside, inducing White to punish the ostensibly neglected king. That the target has survived after being flushed out and then scurrying over to a7 should therefore be in Black's favour, as he can now claim to have emerged from the excitement with a material lead and the prospect of putting the extra major piece to good use. White has dominated the proceedings yet thus far failed to complete the mission. Of course this is not important in the wider sense but, in practical terms, is a significant factor. White is doing perfectly fine on the board when we take a clinical, uninvolved look at the position, but during a game like this, where the roles have been clearly established, there is a tendency for the aggressor to continue to play 'in character' when a shift in gear is necessary. This is borne out in Marin's continued aggression.

24 Bg7?

Having gone this far White's reluctance to take his foot off the pedal results in reckless aggression. There is no denying White's positional superiority, a by-product of the initiative that should have been addressed with 24 Nd5 Bxd5 25 exd5, e.g. 25...Rb7 26 Rb1! Rxb1+ 27 Bxb1 Qb7 28 Bf5 (Marin), which looks good for White, or 25...Qg8 26 Kg2 Bd8 27 Qh5, again with oodles of compensation. The text is exactly the kind of lunge that Black has been waiting for, and indeed the kind of mistake we are more likely to witness in such circumstances.

NOTE: An advantage of provocative defence is the opposition's tendency to feel increasingly obliged to attack when such measures are no longer warranted.

24...Be8 25 Nd5

The alternative is 25 Qxe7 Rxe7 26 Bxh8 Bh5 27 Bxf6 when, after 27...Rxe6 28 Bxe6 Bxd1 29 Nxd1 (29 Bd5 Qf8) 29...Qxe4 Black threatens both ...Qe1+ and ...Qg6, winning a piece. Notice how easily the queen suddenly springs to life here from the experimental post on a8.

25...Bxf7

25...Rb7 26 Qxe7 Rxe7 27 Bxh8 helps White.

26 Nxc7 Qg8! (Diagram 29)

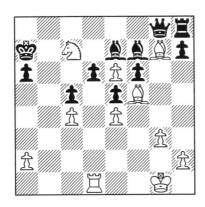

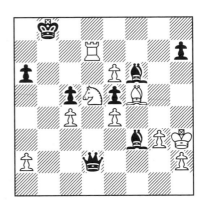

Diagram 29	Diagram 30
Position after 26...Qg8!	Position after 33...Kb8

I would imagine that Ionescu enjoyed this game from start to finish, not least because his play has had an air of the beginner about it. In reality, however, it has been a very good display of practical chess, with an emphasis on psychology. The sharp-eyed amongst you will have noticed that 14...Nc5 is the furthest Black has ventured, yet here he is, continuing with the unconventional theme by operating along the back rank, about to claim a decisive lead.

27 Bxh8 Bh5 28 Bxf6 Bxf6 29 Rxd6 Qg5

Setting up the deciding invasion by the hitherto dormant queen.

30 Nd5 Qc1+ 31 Kg2 Qd2+ 32 Kh3

32 Kg1 Be2! and mate soon follows.

32...Bf3 33 Rd7+ Kb8 0-1 (Diagram 30)

Despite (or because of?) Black's skating on thin ice with his own king, it will emerge as the last one standing now. After 34 Nf4 Qe1 35 Ng2 Qe2 the noose tightens.

Index of Games